# Introduction:
# Welcome to the Western Pennsylvania Birding Trail Guide

One of the great challenges of putting together a list of birding locations is that, unlike most other lists, there's no guarantee that the subjects (the birds themselves) will actually be there when you arrive. Fortunately, for most birders, the search is almost as important as the actual sighting!

The Western Pennsylvania Birding Trail Guide was developed to help birders – experienced or new – and nature lovers of all types to better understand and appreciate the wide range of birding opportunities throughout western Pennsylvania. It is also a companion guide to the Susquehanna River Birding & Wildlife Trail Guide and the Eastern Pennsylvania Birding & Wildlife Guide that cover the central and eastern sections of the state respectively.

From the shores of Lake Erie through the mountain ridges of the Alleghenies and along the many miles of stream and riverbanks throughout the entire region, western PA boasts a tremendous variety of habitats that provide many opportunities to search for wildlife.

And while we can't guarantee that you will find the birds you are after, we do know that any day spent outside birding is better than a day spent indoors.

*Happy Birding!*

# How to Identify Birds

Many bird watchers rely on field marks to identify birds. Field marks are the physical colors and patterns found on a bird during its normal activities. Aside from bill and feet shape, some common field marks may include:

- Eyebrow stripe (also called superciliary, line over the eye)
- Eyeline (line through the eye)
- Whisker mark (also called mustache or malar stripe)
- Wingbars (stripes across the wing)
- Primaries (the long flight feathers on the outer half of the wing)
- Secondaries (the flight feathers on the inner half of the wing)
- Speculum (the patch of colored secondaries that helps identify many ducks)

Many birders state their observations out loud to make a mental note of what they've seen—or to share information with other birders. This can be helpful later when you're using a field guide to identify the birds you've seen.

Some other important things that may help with bird identification include:

**Habitat:** Is the bird in a stand of conifers or an open farm field? Was it in the canopy or foraging on the ground? By observing where the bird is located, you may be able to narrow down the species.

**Behavior:** Observing a bird's behavior is valuable to its identification. Is it clinging to the side of a tree? Or is it foraging on the ground?

**Size:** Comparing the size of the bird you are looking at to the size of a bird you are familiar with can be helpful. Is it bigger or smaller than a robin? Is it bigger or smaller than a crow?

**Shape**: A bird's shape may help you narrow down what group of birds it belongs to. Does it have long legs? Large, broad wings? A thick bill?

**Calls:** Many birds have very different and distinct calls and songs. Recordings of these songs are readily available for study and can help you identify the birds in the area without getting a clear look at them.

# External Anatomy of a Bird

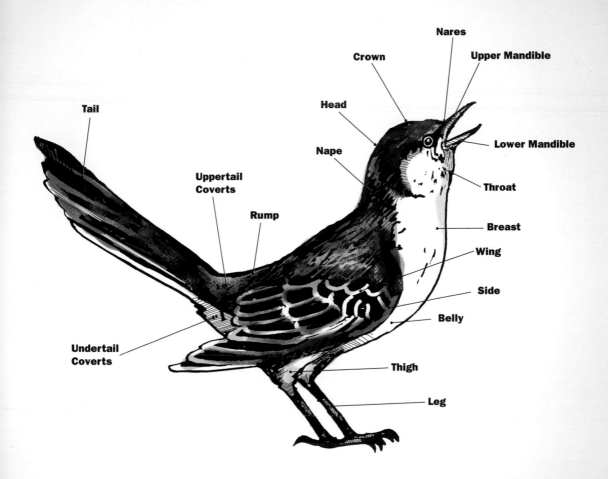

# Making the Most of Your Birding

To make the most out of your birding, it's important to have the proper equipment. Suggested equipment might include:

**Optics:** Optics vary in size and shape. When purchasing binoculars, please consider the weight, the size, and the intended use. Binoculars are usually described with two numbers, such as: 8 x 40 or 10 x 42. The first number is how many times the binocular magnifies what you're looking at. Most birders use 7x, 8x, or 10x binoculars. The second number is the diameter, in millimeters, of the large objective lenses through which light enters the binocular. The larger the diameter, the better the binoculars function in low light situations. Spotting scopes may also be used to get a close-up look at birds such as waterfowl or shorebirds in open areas.

**Clothing:** Pennsylvania hosts many different kinds of weather conditions and many kinds of insects and ticks in the field. Please remember to dress appropriately for the location and the weather. A hat will help to block out the sun and keep you warmer on cold days. Long pants and long sleeves, paired with light colors, will help discourage ticks and mosquitoes. Layering is a good technique when starting out early in the day. Remember to wear blaze orange clothing during hunting seasons!

**Water and Snacks:** Staying hydrated is essential to any good experience in the field. Remember to bring snacks and water with you, even during cold weather.

**Field Guides:** A portable field guide is key to a great experience. A good guide gives details on color and plumage patterns and is easily accessible in the field.

**Notebook and Pencil:** Bring along a notebook and pencil so you have a place to write sightings and copy down any field marks or habitat notes.

**Checklist:** It's helpful to bring along a checklist of the birds expected in the area you will be visiting.

**Smart Phones:** Many smart phones and smart devices have applications that are well suited for bird watching. Some applications are field guides—complete with pictures and audio bird recordings. Others are better suited for audio recording your own notes or reporting your sightings directly from the field.

# Potential Hazards

Whenever you participate in an outdoor activity such as birding, it is important to be aware of the potential hazards that may be avoided with proper planning. Always know your limitations and make sure someone knows where you are going and when you will be returning. Carry a map, compass, and cell phone—many newer models may contain GPS that could help if you are lost but keep in mind that not all areas have cell phone reception.

All of the natural areas in this guide are home to a diversity of plants and wildlife. Learn to identify the natural hazards that are present in an area, such as poison ivy and poison sumac. Black bears are active year-round and common throughout Pennsylvania. Be aware that ticks are present in many of these birding locations and may carry Lyme disease. Consider applying a product containing DEET and always check for ticks upon your return from the field.

*Black Bear - Courtesy of Fotosearch*

*Sunset at Bald Knob*

# Finding Birds in the Region:

The Western Pennsylvania Bird List, which begins on page 104 of this guide, represents most species that have occurred within the region. It is not intended to be an exhaustive or historical list of occurrence.

Each species has been assigned one of the following qualifiers: regular, casual, or accidental. These terms are provided to illustrate the likelihood that the species can be found within the entire region and not at a specific site. Please refer to the bird list provided for each site to determine the likelihood and timing of finding a species at a specific site.

# Bird List Qualifiers:

**Regular:** this species can be found in appropriate habitat and within season throughout the region.

**Casual:** this species can be found in appropriate habitat and within season, but infrequently throughout the region.

**Accidental:** this species has been recorded only a few times within the region. Its appearance may have been due to a migration error or strong weather patterns.

# Make it a Day– Birding Loops

While using this guide, consider combining a couple of nearby locations to make best use of your location and wildlife watching opportunities. For all-day wildlife watching opportunities, the following are a few suggestions of Western Pennsylvania loops.

## Southwestern Pennsylvania:

For a great all-day interior forest experience in southwestern Pennsylvania, begin in Allegheny County at Harrison Hills Park. The park hosts an amazing array of migrants in May, and several key interior forest birds remain throughout the breeding season. Generally speaking, the "Meadow Trail" in the center of the park along a small stream, and Rachel Carson Trail, along the south ridge of the park are best.

From Harrison Hills Park, visit the Butler to Freeport Community Trail in Butler County, only 10 minutes away. Again, this location can be teeming with migrants in season. The steep forested valleys coupled with floodplains along Buffalo Creek provide a diversity of habitat for breeding species.

One and one-half miles from the Butler to Freeport Community Trail is Audubon Society of Western Pennsylvania's Todd Nature Reserve. The reserve is cut by several streams, and the cool hemlock-lined valleys are a refreshing break during warm afternoon temperatures. Louisiana Waterthrush, Black-throated Green Warbler and Acadian Flycatcher are almost ubiquitous at this reserve.

At the completion of this loop, you are only 10 miles from your starting location at Harrison Hills Park. All three locations are part of the Buffalo Creek Valley Important Bird Area.

## Western Pennsylvania:

For a good all-day experience in late fall or winter in western Pennsylvania, begin in Lawrence County. Approximately one and one-half hours north of Pittsburgh are the Volant Strips and nearby Pennsy and Black Swamps.

Pennsy Swamp is crossed on the way to Volant. A stop along the road at this small swamp can produce waterfowl and wading birds. Red-headed Woodpeckers are occasionally seen in the area as well. Viewing is done from the roadside, so be aware of oncoming traffic.

A few miles from Pennsy Swamp are the Volant Strips. The fields along this stretch of road can produce excellent views of Short-eared Owl, Northern Harrier,

American Kestrel, Sandhill Crane, and a slew of grassland sparrows. Drive the roads slowly and stop frequently, scanning the fields as you go. Remember to pull off of the road where possible, as not to block traffic.

Black Swamp is also only a mile from the Volant fields. Hidden in a patch of woodland, Black Swamp has produced a few rare birds such as American White Pelican. The parking area for Black Swamp is a dirt road, which may be difficult to pass in spring and fall. Drive carefully and park at the end of the road. The pines surrounding the parking lot are often a good place to watch for passerines and owls. The swamp is just beyond the parking area, and a small trail leads along the edge of the swamp.

If you've carefully birded this area, it should be nearing lunchtime. Return to I-79 and spend your afternoon at Moraine Lake State Park. Waterfowl are plentiful on the lake in late fall and winter. Scoters, loons, mergansers and a long list of ducks are common.

Sandhill Cranes

## Northwestern Pennsylvania:

Another great all-day loop in the northern section of this region includes several favorite locations of local birdwatchers during migration.

Begin at the Fish Hatchery in Crawford County and spend some time watching the ponds at the site. Continue on to the Wildlife Learning Center at Pymatuning Lake. The upland and woodland areas surrounding the center can produce a good list of migrating passerines. Also while at the Learning Center, scan the propagation section of Pymatuning Lake. Bald Eagles nest in the area and gulls are often numerous.

Although not contained as a site in this guide, the nearby spillway at Pymatuning Lake, only 0.1 mile from the Learning Center, provides an opportunity to scan the larger waters of the lake. Expect waterfowl and gulls in migration.

From the spillway, continue on to Miller's Pond, a site that often attracts an array of shorebirds in spring and fall. Scan each of the ponds, paying particular attention to the banks or shallows. If you do this loop in late fall or early winter, look for Rough-legged Hawks.

Finish this loop at Hartstown Marsh. The marsh can contain just about anything in migration, including eagles, waterfowl, and wading birds. The woodland areas around the marsh provide good stopover habitat for passerines.

# American Birding Association's Code of Birding Ethics

Everyone who enjoys birds and birding must always respect wildlife, the environment, and the rights of others. In any conflict of interest between birds and birders, the welfare of the birds and their environment comes first. Audubon Society of Western Pennsylvania unconditionally endorses the American Birding Association's Code of Birding Ethics and encourages all people, whether birding alone or in a group, to follow these guiding principles:

**1.** Promote the welfare of birds and their environment.

**1 (a)** Support the protection of important bird habitat.

**1 (b)** To avoid stressing birds or exposing them to danger, exercise restraint and caution during observation, photography, sound recording, or filming. Limit the use of recordings and other methods of attracting birds, and never use such methods in heavily birded areas or for attracting any species that is Threatened, Endangered, or of Special Concern, or is rare in your local area.

Keep well back from nests and nesting colonies, roosts, display areas, and important feeding sites. In such sensitive areas, if there is a need for extended observation, photography, filming, or recording, try to use a blind or hide, and take advantage of natural cover. Use artificial light sparingly for filming or photography, especially for close-ups.

**1 (c)** Before advertising the presence of a rare bird, evaluate the potential for disturbance to the bird, its surroundings, and other people in the area, and proceed only if access can be controlled, disturbance can be minimized, and permission has been obtained from private land-owners. The sites of rare nesting birds should be divulged only to the proper conservation authorities.

**1 (d)** Stay on roads, trails, and paths where they exist; otherwise keep habitat disturbance to a minimum.

**2.** Respect the law and the rights of others.

**2 (a)** Do not enter private property without the owner's explicit permission.

**2 (b)** Follow all laws, rules, and regulations governing use of roads and public areas, both at home and abroad.

**2 (c)** Practice common courtesy in contacts with other people. Your exemplary behavior will generate goodwill with birders and non-birders alike.

**3.** Ensure that feeders, nest structures, and other artificial bird environments are safe.

**3 (a)** Keep dispensers, water, and food clean and free of decay or disease. It is important to feed birds continually during harsh weather.

**3 (b)** Maintain and clean nest structures regularly.

**3 (c)** If you are attracting birds to an area, ensure the birds are not exposed to predation from cats and other domestic animals, or dangers posed by artificial hazards.

**4.** Group birding, whether organized or impromptu, requires special care. Each individual in the group, in addition to the obligations spelled out in Items #1 and #2, has responsibilities as a Group Member.

**4 (a)** Respect the interests, rights, and skills of fellow birders, as well as those of people participating in other legitimate outdoor activities. Freely share your knowledge and experience, except where code 1(c) applies. Be especially helpful to beginning birders.

**4 (b)** If you witness unethical birding behavior, assess the situation and intervene if you think it prudent. When interceding, inform the person(s) of the inappropriate action and attempt, within reason, to have it stopped. If the behavior continues, document it and notify appropriate individuals or organizations.

Group Leader Responsibilities
(amateur and professional trips and tours):

**4 (c)** Be an exemplary ethical role model for the group. Teach through word and example.

**4 (d)** Keep groups to a size that limits impact on the environment and does not interfere with others using the same area.

**4 (e)** Ensure everyone in the group knows of and practices this code.

**4 (f)** Learn and inform the group of any special circumstances applicable to the areas being visited (e.g., no tape recorders allowed).

**4 (g)** Acknowledge that professional tour companies bear a special responsibility to place the welfare of birds and the benefits of public knowledge ahead of the company's commercial interests. Ideally, leaders should keep track of tour sightings, document unusual occurrences, and submit records to appropriate organizations.

*\* Ethics code created and developed by the American Birding Association*

*Photo courtesy of Brian Shema*

# National Aviary

America's premier zoo dedicated to birds, the National Aviary is home to a diverse collection of more than 700 birds representing 200 species, many of them threatened or endangered in the wild. The National Aviary's large walk-through exhibits allow for intimate, up-close interactions between visitors and free-flying birds. Daily programs are designed to be interactive, educational and fun, with many opportunities to hand-feed and learn about species rarely found in zoos.

Penguin Point, an open air exhibit that is home to a colony of African penguins, allows up-close views of the penguins swimming, playing, and basking in the sun, while the new Grasslands Exhibit places guests in a light-filled space inhabited by finches, weavers, doves, and other fragile but beautiful birds.

Special private encounters in which guests join Aviary trainers in one-on-one interactions with select birds can be arranged in advance, including Flamingo Connection, Penguin Connection, and Raptor Experience.

The National Aviary's daily programming also includes shows in the FliteZone™ Theater, opened in fall 2010. The FliteZone Theater is the first theater designed specifically for presenting indoor free-flight bird shows. In this space, an array of species, including vultures, macaws, owls, eagles and more demonstrate remarkable natural behaviors as they fly over and stroll among seated guests. Lure-flying demonstrations on the new rooftop Sky Deck will give guests the opportunity to see birds of prey catching food in mid air.

### Plan your trip:
National Aviary
Allegheny Commons West
700 Arch Street
Pittsburgh, PA 15212
412-323-7235 or aviary.org

Photos courtesy of the National Aviary

# Presque Isle State Park

Presque Isle State Park is a major recreational destination in northwestern Pennsylvania, attracting nearly four million visitors each year. As Pennsylvania's only "seashore," Presque Isle offers its visitors a beautiful coastline and many recreational activities, including birding, swimming, boating, fishing, hiking, bicycling, and in-line skating.

The park has the enviable distinction of being the only surf beach in the state of Pennsylvania. A recurring sand spit peninsula that juts out into Lake Erie, the park's location makes it a favorite spot for observing the area's bird migration, geological diversity, biological diversity, and historical significance.

The gateway to Presque Isle is the Tom Ridge Environmental Center (TREC). An educational center offering environmental programming, TREC is dedicated to teaching visitors about Presque Isle and the many different forms of life that inhabit this unique peninsula. TREC also serves as a center for research, contributing to conservation efforts and promoting environmental awareness. There is free admission to the interactive exhibits and the 75-foot observation tower.

A National Natural Landmark, Presque Isle contains a greater number of the state's endangered, threatened and rare species than any other area of comparable size in Pennsylvania. Many nature lovers experience the park by hiking the 11 miles of trails or by riding the 14-mile paved Karl Boyes Multi-purpose National Recreation Trail.

The neck of the peninsula is attached to the mainland four miles west of downtown Erie, Pennsylvania. The park creates Presque Isle Bay, a wide and deep harbor for the city of Erie, that attracts both pleasure boats and worldwide freighters, making Erie an important Great Lakes shipping port.

## Plan your trip:

Presque Isle State Park
301 Peninsula Drive, Suite 1
Erie, PA 16505-2042
www.dcnr.state.pa.us/stateparks/parks/presqueisle.aspx

White-crowned Sparrow

Horned Grebe

# Powdermill Nature Reserve

Powdermill Nature Reserve was established in 1956 to serve as a field station of Carnegie Museum of Natural History for long-term studies of natural populations—their life histories, behaviors, and ecological relationships. More than 200 different species of birds stop at Powdermill for a rest during their migration.

Today, the reserve is far more beautiful than when it was established, due to the natural growth of protected vegetation and the efforts of many supporters. Powdermill has recently undergone a significant expansion and upgrade including technologies that are energy efficient, are derived from renewable resources, and that effectively manage wastewater. The building's centerpiece is a simulated wetlands Marsh Machine wastewater treatment system—and other green technologies include straw bale insulation, recycled paper wallboards, and carpets made of truck tires. A freestanding 800 square foot solar powered house, designed by architecture and engineering students at Carnegie Mellon University and the University of Pittsburgh, is an onsite exhibit.

Powdermill Nature Reserve offers many opportunities for people of all ages to experience the beauty of the Laurel Highlands through its hiking trails, educational programs, and changing exhibitions. Families may attend free nature programs on Sundays from January through October and nature programs for children are run during the summer.

The reserve is used by scientists to monitor and study changes in the local ecology and wildlife populations. It has served as a refuge for many plants and animals now becoming increasingly rare in our region as their habitats are destroyed. Powdermill Run, the mountain spring stream that traverses the mixed deciduous forest property, was found to be one of the very few unpolluted streams available for ongoing studies of aquatic life.

The well-known avian research at Powdermill was started by senior bird bander Robert Leberman in 1961. Together with Field Ornithologist Robert S. Mulvihill and a string of dedicated volunteers, Powdermill has banded an average of about 10,000 birds annually over the course of the program's history. Powdermill's bird-banding database currently contains over a half million records representing almost 200 species.

Because virtually all of these data have been collected either by Robert Leberman and Robert Mulvihill, Powdermill's large bird-banding and recapture database may well be the most internally consistent of its kind. From this collected data, knowledge has been gained about longevity in wild bird populations, differences between sexes and age groups in migration behavior, bird life cycles, and weight and plumage changes.

## Plan your trip:

Powdermill Nature Reserve
1847 Route 381
Rector, PA 15677
724-593-4040 or powdermill.org

*White-winged Crossbill*

# Carnegie Museum of Natural History

The Carnegie Museum of Natural History is home to an extraordinary collection of mounted bird specimens. The museum's exhibits—especially in Bird Hallway and the second floor dioramas—are a great venue to see the diversity in birds.

The upper portions of Bird Hallway contain displays of the world's birds, mounted over the past two centuries. Specimens include Endangered and Extinct Species, Flightlessness, Tropical Rainforests, Birds of Paradise, Sexual Dimorphism, Avian Reproduction, Aquatic Birds, Adaptations for Feeding, and Defining Species. The lower hallway has displays of many non-passerines found in Pennsylvania including ducks, raptors, herons, doves, and shorebirds.

Botany Hall's dioramas recreate natural habitats of Pennsylvania's native birds. Highlights include a Lake Erie Shoreline, a Pennsylvania Bog, Northern Hardwood Forest, and Spring Flora. An upgrade to the North American Hall incorporated birds into the large mammal dioramas. Each of these areas allow individuals to vividly imagine visiting the artfully depicted landscapes

## Plan your trip:
Carnegie Museum of Natural History
4400 Forbes Avenue
Pittsburgh, PA 15213
412-622-3309

*Red-winged Blackbird*

# Allegheny County

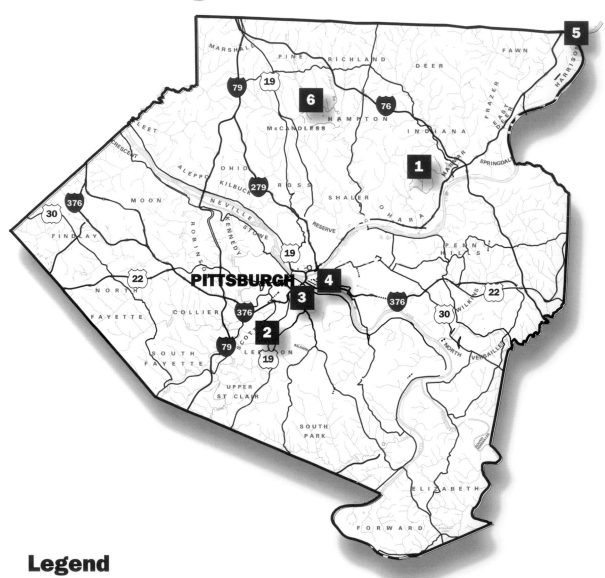

**Legend**

 Handicapped Accessibility

 Hiking Trails

 Biking Trails

 Restrooms

Dogs Allowed

# 1 BEECHWOOD FARMS NATURE RESERVE

**Location:** Beechwood Farms Nature Reserve is located in Allegheny County, in the Borough of Fox Chapel.

**Owner/Manager:** Audubon Society of Western Pennsylvania

**GPS Coordinates:** 40° 32' 30" N, 79° 54' 18" W

**Directions, Access, & Parking:** From Pittsburgh take PA-28 north to Exit 5B, PA-8 north/Butler. At the first traffic light, turn right onto Kittanning Road. Continue on Kittanning Road for 4.5 miles; it will become Dorseyville Road without any notification. Beechwood Farms will be on your left. Parking is available for cars and buses. Some facilities are handicapped accessible.

**Site Description:** The 134-acre Beechwood Farms Nature Reserve is the headquarters of Audubon Society of Western Pennsylvania. The reserve is home to five miles of trails through deciduous, coniferous, and early successional forests, shrub/scrub, pond, and stream areas.

**Site Information:** Free admission. On-site trails, information, observation deck, visitor center, restrooms, drinking water, guided tours, environmental education programs, education classrooms, Audubon Nature Store, Teacher Resource Center, Natural History Library, and Audubon Center for Native Plants are all available. The conservation department maintains a seasonal bird checklist viewable in the nature store. Archery hunting is allowed by permit only. Lodging, restaurants, gasoline, and convenience/grocery stores are all nearby.

**Key Birds and Wildlife:** Red-bellied Woodpecker, Pileated Woodpecker, Red-tailed Hawk, Black-capped Chickadee, Carolina Chickadee, White-breasted Nuthatch, Red-shouldered Hawk, Scarlet Tanager, Indigo Bunting, Yellow Warbler, Baltimore Oriole, Hooded Warbler, Northern Flicker, Brown Creeper. Twenty-six species of warblers can be found during spring migration. An exceptional diversity of dragonflies and damselflies appear at the pond in season.

**Other Comments:** Beechwood Farms Nature Reserve allows for wildlife observation and nature study while still in close proximity to downtown Pittsburgh and its northern suburbs. Visit www.aswp.org for more information.

**Contact Information:**
Beechwood Farms Nature Reserve
614 Dorseyville Road
Pittsburgh, PA 15238
(412) 963-6100

Hooded Warbler

# 2 BOYCE MAYVIEW PARK

**Location:** Boyce Mayview Park is located in the township of Upper St. Clair, in southwestern Allegheny County.

**Owner/Manager:** Township of Upper St. Clair/ Township of Upper St. Clair Department of Recreation and Leisure

**GPS Coordinates:** 40° 18′ 55″ N, 80° 5′ 58″ W

**Directions, Access, & Parking:** From Pittsburgh take US-19/Washington Road south to Boyce Road. Turn right and proceed 0.5 miles to the intersection with Morton Road on the right. Turn right and then immediately left into the garden plot parking area. There is ample parking and easy access for cars and buses.

**Site Description:** The 475-acre Boyce Mayview Park contains deciduous forest, shrub/scrub, grassland/savanna, swamp, wetlands, and stream areas. The park consists of extensive woodlands, fields, and open spaces as well as stream valleys, all interwoven with well-marked hiking and biking trails. The majority of the natural areas are located in the southern portion of the park. Community residents have vegetable garden plots, a recreation center, nature center, swimming pool, and baseball/softball and soccer/football fields mostly clustered in the northern part of the park. Chartiers Creek and the extensive wetlands lie on the western boundary of the property. This provides diverse habitat for waterfowl, birds, plants, and other wildlife.

**Site Information:** Free admission. On-site trails that vary from easy to moderate, an observation deck, and a nature center are on the property. Restaurants, gasoline, and convenience/grocery stores are located nearby.

**Key Birds and Wildlife:** Sharp-shinned Hawk, Red-tailed Hawk, Chimney Swift, Belted Kingfisher, Red-bellied Woodpecker, Hairy Woodpecker, Northern Flicker, Eastern Phoebe, Carolina Chickadee, Red-breasted Nuthatch, White-breasted Nuthatch, Brown Creeper, Carolina Wren, Cedar Waxwing, Red-eyed Vireo, Magnolia Warbler, Black-throated Blue Warbler, Black-throated Green Warbler, Blackpoll Warbler, American Redstart, Rose-breasted Grosbeak, Eastern Towhee, Song Sparrow, Eastern Bluebird, Great Blue Heron. Over 150 species of birds, 200 species of plants, and 55 species of butterflies have been observed in the park.

**Other Comments:** In 1996 about 238 acres of the Mayview Farm property were acquired from the state and combined with the 236-acre Boyce Park to form Boyce Mayview Park. The master plan calls for keeping 86 percent of the park largely undeveloped. Visit www.twpusc.org/rec/parks/boycemay for more information.

**Contact Information:**
Township of Upper St. Clair Recreation Department
1551 Mayview Road
Upper St. Clair, PA 15241
(412) 221-1099

Long-tailed Duck

Red-winged Blackbird

## 3 DUCK HOLLOW

**Location:** Duck Hollow is located in Allegheny County on Old Browns Hill Road, in the City of Pittsburgh. Duck Hollow is the area where Nine Mile Run flows into the Monongahela River.

**Owner/Manager:** City of Pittsburgh/Pittsburgh Department of Public Works in cooperation with Pittsburgh Parks Conservancy and Nine Mile Run Watershed Association

**GPS Coordinates:** 40° 24' 50" N, 79° 55' 1" W

**Directions, Access, & Parking:** From downtown Pittsburgh take I-376 E to Exit 5/Homestead. Merge onto Beechwood Boulevard, which becomes Browns Hill Road. Turn left onto Old Browns Hill Road, then right at the dead end of McFarren Street. Parking is available for cars and buses.

**Site Description:** Duck Hollow is home to riparian, river, and stream areas. It is also one of a limited number of access sites where the Monongahela River can be viewed up close.

**Site Information:** Free admission. Duck Hollow Trail is part of the Great Allegheny Passage trail system. Fishing is permitted. Lodging, restaurants, gas stations, and convenience/grocery stores are all nearby.

**Key Birds and Wildlife:** Belted Kingfisher, Pied-billed Grebe, Bufflehead, Lesser Scaup, Ring-necked Duck, Northern Rough-winged Swallow, Baltimore Oriole, Yellow Warbler, Orchard Oriole, Warbling Vireo. Brant, Forster's Tern, Horned Grebe, and Peregrine Falcon have been found at the site in recent years.

**Other Comments:** The adjacent Nine Mile Run Watershed encompasses 6.5 square miles and is a remarkable example of urban stream restoration. Visit www.ninemilerun.org/birds for more information.

**Contact Information:**
Dept. of Public Works, Division #3
88 Swinburne Street
Pittsburgh, PA 15207
(412) 255-0768

Pittsburgh Parks Conservancy
2000 Technology Drive, Suite 300
Pittsburgh, PA 15219
(412) 682-7275

Nine Mile Run Watershed Association
702 South Trenton Avenue
Pittsburgh, PA 15221
(412) 371-8779

*Ring-necked Duck*

*Olive-sided Flycatcher*

# 4 FRICK PARK

**Location:** Frick Park, in Allegheny County, is located in the Squirrel Hill/Regent Square section of Pittsburgh.

**Owner/Manager:** City of Pittsburgh/Pittsburgh Department of Public Works in cooperation with Pittsburgh Parks Conservancy

**GPS Coordinates:** 40° 25' 56" N, 79° 54' 17" W (Fern Hollow Entrance); 40° 26' 11" N, 79° 54' 30" W

**Directions, Access, & Parking:** Fern Hollow Entrance: From downtown Pittsburgh take I-376 E to Exit 7/Edgewood. Follow the signs to S. Braddock Avenue and drive north 0.3 miles to W. Hutchinson Avenue. Turn left and drive 0.2 miles to Lancaster Avenue. Turn right and follow the park entrance driveway to the parking lot at the bottom of the hill. Parking is available for cars and buses. Beechwood Boulevard Entrance: From downtown Pittsburgh, take I-376 E to Exit 5/Squirrel Hill/Homestead. Go 0.2 miles, then turn left onto Forward Avenue/Squirrel Hill. Go 0.3 miles. At the five-way intersection, make a slight right to stay on Forward Avenue. Go 0.4 miles and turn left at the light at the top of the hill onto Beechwood Boulevard. Continue 0.8 miles to the park entrance on the right. Parking is available for cars and buses.

**Site Description:** The 600-acre Frick Park is primarily deciduous and early successional forests, shrub/scrub, and stream areas, with several extensive, restored wetlands. Nine Mile Run runs across and through the southern part of the park. Most of the playgrounds and heavily manicured areas are on the periphery, leaving a core of wooded hills and ravines.

**Site Information:** Free admission. The park has approximately 10 miles of trails. An environmental center, information, portable restrooms, and drinking water (warm months) are available. Other features include baseball fields, a playground, tennis courts, and a lawn bowling court. Lodging, restaurants, gasoline, and convenience stores are nearby.

**Key Birds and Wildlife:** In migration: Winter Wren, Blue-headed Vireo, Black-throated Green Warbler, Killdeer, Spotted Sandpiper, Red-eyed Vireo, American Redstart, Common Yellowthroat, Chipping Sparrow, Savannah Sparrow, Purple Finch. Breeding: Baltimore and Orchard Orioles, Cooper's Hawk, Indigo Bunting, Pileated Woodpecker. Frick Park is an excellent migrant trap in the east end of Pittsburgh. During spring and fall migration, many birds utilize the woods as a feeding and resting area.

**Other Comments:** Henry Clay Frick, a millionaire industrialist, bequeathed 151 acres and $2 million to the City of Pittsburgh in 1919 to help create and maintain a park. The park has been expanded with acquisitions of adjacent lands over the years. Future plans include building a new Environmental Center in order to create a hub for environmental education in Pittsburgh. Visit www.pittsburghparks.org for more information.

**Contact Information:**
Frick Environmental Center
2005 Beechwood Boulevard
Pittsburgh, PA 15217
(412) 422-6538

# 5 HARRISON HILLS PARK

**Location:** Harrison Hills Park is located in Allegheny County, near the town of Natrona Heights.

**Owner/Manager:** Allegheny County/Allegheny County Parks Department

**GPS Coordinates:** 40° 39' 12" N, 79° 42' 27" W

**Directions, Access, & Parking:** From Pittsburgh take PA-28 north to Exit 16. Turn right and travel 0.6 miles to Freeport Road. Turn right and travel 0.6 miles to the park entrance on the left. Parking for cars and buses is available. Some areas are handicapped accessible.

**Site Description:** The park covers 500 acres and contains deciduous and early successional forests, shrub/scrub areas, fallow fields, marsh, riparian, pond, river, and stream areas. Harrison Hills Park has over 60 species of trees. Harrison Hills Park is part of the Buffalo Creek Valley Important Bird Area #22.

**Site Information:** Free admission. The park is open for day use only. The county park has 14 miles of bridle, hiking, walking/jogging, and mountain biking trails. Ten percent of the Rachel Carson Trail is a part of this park's trail system. Self-guided trails, environmental education center, restrooms, drinking water, interpretive signage, and a deck to view the Allegheny River from 400 feet above the water are available. The park allows horseback riding and mountain biking, which have a low impact on birding and birders. There is also a soccer field used on the weekend. Hunting is allowed. Restaurants, gasoline, convenience/grocery stores, and lodging are located within a 5-mile drive.

**Key Birds and Wildlife:** Pileated Woodpecker, Eastern Wood-Pewee, Philadelphia Vireo, Kentucky Warbler, Louisiana Waterthrush, Song Sparrow. Harrison Hills Park is one of the few places in Allegheny County with breeding Worm-eating Warblers and is known for its population of Cerulean Warblers. There is an effort under way to attract a breeding colony of Purple Martins. This site boasts fantastic spring and fall migration bird-watching opportunities; over 180 species of birds have been identified within the park. Fox Squirrel, Eastern Cottontail, and American Toad are found here.

**Other Comments:** The entrance gate is opened at 8am. Harrison Hills Park occupies the extreme northeast portion of Allegheny County, bordering the Allegheny River and offering a magnificent overlook of Westmoreland, Butler, and Armstrong counties. Visit www.alleghenycounty.us/parks/hhfac.aspx for more information.

**Contact Information:**
Harrison Hills Park
5200 Freeport Road
Natrona Heights, PA 15065
(724) 295-3570

*Black-and-white Warbler*

*Cape May Warbler*

# 6 NORTH PARK LATODAMI ENVIRONMENTAL EDUCATION CENTER

**Location:** North Park's Latodami Environmental Education Center is located in Allegheny County, near the town of Wexford.

**Owner/Manager:** Allegheny County/Allegheny County Parks Department

**GPS Coordinates:** 40° 37' 10" N, 80° 1' 49" W

**Directions, Access, & Parking:** Take I-79 N to Exit 73/Wexford. Turn right onto PA-910 and drive for 3.9 miles to Pearce Mill Road. Turn right on Pearce Mill Road and continue 0.6 miles to Brown Road. Turn right on Brown Road. The entrance to the Environmental Education Center is located on the right at 575 Brown Road. Parking is available for cars and buses, and the venue is handicapped accessible. Check additional birding sites in the North Park at Erie, Gold Star, and Point Groves on Lake Shore Drive, Marshall Island on Pearce Mill Road, and the trails behind Pie Traynor Field.

**Site Description:** The 3,400-acre North Park is home to deciduous, coniferous, mixed, and early successional forests, shrub/scrub, fallow fields, marsh, riparian, lake, pond, stream, and wetland areas. Latodami has been designated as an Important Mammal Area.

**Site Information:** Free admission. Fourteen short and interconnected trails, information, an observation deck, an observation blind, a visitor center, restrooms, drinking water, interpretive signage, guided tours, environmental education, and custom programs are all available around Latodami Environmental Education Center. Biking, mountain biking, horseback riding, canoeing/kayaking, and organized sports are permitted in North Park. Limited archery hunting takes place in the park.

**Key Birds and Wildlife:** Barred Owl, Green Heron, Great Blue Heron, Tree Swallow, Eastern Bluebird, Baltimore Oriole, Orchard Oriole. In the spring 234 breeding and/or migratory birds have been documented in the area, including 14 species of warblers. Waterfowl and shorebirds can be spotted on Latodami's pond as well as on Marshall Lake and North Park Lake. Herring Gulls are often seen on North Park Lake. Wood frog, eastern American toad, northern green frog, northern dusky salamander, American beaver, little brown bat, and Virginia opossum are in the park.

**Other Comments:** In 2009 an Ecosystem Restoration Project began with the draining of 60-acre North Park Lake. Silt and sediment had been building up in the lake since 1936. The two-year project will restore the lake to a depth of 24 feet. Visit www.latodami.org for more information.

**Contact Information:**
Latodami Environmental Center
575 Brown Road
Wexford, PA 15090
(724) 935-2170

Green Heron

*Red-winged Blackbird*

# Armstrong County

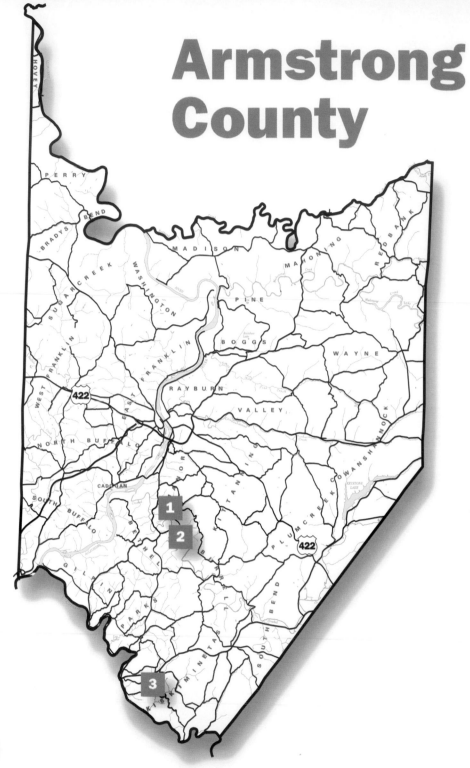

## Legend

 Handicapped Accessibility

 Hiking Trails

 Biking Trails

 Restrooms

 Dogs Allowed

# 1 CROOKED CREEK ENVIRONMENTAL LEARNING CENTER

**Location:** Crooked Creek Environmental Learning Center is located in Armstrong County, near the town of Ford City.

**Owner/Manager:** Leased to the Armstrong Educational Trust by United States Army Corps of Engineers

**GPS Coordinates:** 40° 42' 57" N, 79° 31' 0" W

**Directions, Access, & Parking:** From the Kittanning/Ford City area, take PA-66 south for 6 miles. Turn left onto Crooked Creek Dam Road (SR2019) and travel 0.5 miles. Turn left onto Kerr Road (T670) and travel 0.25 miles. The learning center is at the end of Kerr Road. Parking is available for cars and buses and the venue is handicapped accessible. There are handicapped-accessible fishing piers on Crooked Creek Lake and at the Outflow Recreation Area in the nearby park.

**Site Description:** The 31-acre Crooked Creek Environmental Learning Center contains deciduous, coniferous, and mixed forests; early successional forest, shrub/scrub, swamp, marsh, riparian, lake, pond, and stream areas.

**Site Information:** Crooked Creek Environmental Learning Center offers overnight accommodations for groups. Two buildings house a multipurpose room, dormitory, kitchen, great room with an extensive collection of mounted specimens, a conference room, and office space. An interpretive trail, herb garden, restrooms, drinking water, signage, guided tours, environmental programs, and custom programs are available. Lodging, restaurants, campgrounds, gasoline, and convenience stores are close by.

**Key Birds and Wildlife:** Bald Eagle, Tundra Swan, Great Blue Heron, Pileated Woodpecker, Wood Duck, Baltimore Oriole, Scarlet Tanager, Great Egret, Northern Harrier, Wild Turkey, Osprey, Double-crested Cormorant. Eastern Bluebird nesting boxes are on site. American beavers and white-tailed deer may be seen.

**Other Comments:** This learning center is one of several across the state specifically designed to promote environmental education and resource conservation. The adjacent Crooked Creek Lake with its 2,664 acres can provide all of the activities and amenities of a large state park. Visit www.crookedcreekelc.org for more information.

**Contact Information:**
Crooked Creek Environmental Learning Center
142 Kerr Road
Ford City, PA
(724) 763-6316

Armstrong Educational Trust
81 Glade Drive
Kittanning, PA 16201
(724) 543-2599

*Cooper's Hawk*

*Ruddy Duck*

# 2 CROOKED CREEK LAKE

**Location:** Crooked Creek Lake is located in Armstrong County, southeast of the town of Ford City.

**Owner/Manager:** United States/United States Army Corps of Engineers

**GPS Coordinates:** 40° 42' 49" N, 79° 30' 48" W

**Directions, Access, & Parking:** Crooked Creek Lake is located only 30 miles northeast of Pittsburgh, 8 miles south of Kittanning and 8 miles north of Leechburg on PA-66. To access the park turn onto Crooked Creek Dam Road (SR2019) from PA-66. The park office will be on your right. Parking is available for cars and buses, and the area is handicapped accessible.

**Site Description:** The Crooked Creek Lake park covers 2,664 acres, about 400 acres of which are a narrow lake. The area contains deciduous, coniferous, mixed, and early successional forests, shrub/scrub, cultivated and fallow fields, swamp, wetlands, riparian, lake, pond, river, and stream areas.

**Site Information:** Free admission. Trails, information, visitor center, interpretive trails, handicapped-accessible restrooms, drinking water, dam overlook, handicapped accessible fishing pier, and camping are available. Horseback riding, motorized boating with no horsepower limit, swimming, picnicking, fishing, jet skiing, canoeing/kayaking, and hunting are permitted. Restaurants, gasoline, and convenience/grocery stores are located nearby.

**Key Birds and Wildlife:** Bald Eagle, Belted Kingfisher, Tundra Swan, Great Blue Heron, Pileated Woodpecker, Wood Duck, Eastern Bluebird, Baltimore Oriole, Scarlet Tanager, Great Egret, Northern Harrier, Wild Turkey, Osprey, Double-crested Cormorant, Dark-eyed Junco, Carolina Wren, Red-breasted Merganser, Green Heron, Eastern Phoebe, Red winged Blackbird, Rusty Blackbird, Pine Siskin. Spring and fall are prime times to view wildlife. From Robb's Fording Road, canoes and kayaks may enter the water to permit viewing of eagles and waterfowl in summer and fall. The lake contains large populations of largemouth and smallmouth bass, walleye, and muskie.

**Other Comments:** This area is a flood control reservoir with seasonal use. For daily lake and recreation information, visitors can call a 24-hour recorded message at (724) 763-2764. Information is updated daily from May through September. From October through April, call the Park Office weekdays at (724) 763-3161 for lake and recreation information. Certain areas of the park are closed during the winter months. Visit the Crooked Creek Lake Fact Sheet at www.lrp.usace.army.mil/rec/lakes/crookedc_fact.pdf for more information.

**Contact Information:**
Crooked Creek Lake
114 Park Main Road
Ford City, PA 16226-8815
(724) 763-3161

## 3 ROARING RUN ♿ 🚶 🚲 🚻 🐕
## RECREATION AREA

**Location:** Roaring Run Recreation Area is located along Roaring Run and the Kiskiminetas River in Armstrong County, about 45 miles from Pittsburgh and less than 1 mile from the town of Apollo.

**Owner/Manager:** Roaring Run Watershed Association

**GPS Coordinates:** 40° 33' 52" N, 79° 33' 34" W

**Directions, Access, & Parking:** To access the Roaring Run (main) trailhead, travel on PA-66 to the bridge across the Kiskiminetas River at Apollo. On the Apollo (east) side of the river immediately drive south along the river on Kiski Avenue for 0.75 miles. Stay to the right and low (along the river) when the road becomes Canal Road. Follow Canal Road to the trailhead. Use caution when traveling on Kiski Avenue and Canal Road because these roads are narrow. Parking capacity at the Roaring Run trailhead is 105 vehicles, Rock Furnace allows parking for approximately 10 cars, and Edmon allows for about 30 cars. Buses are welcome here. Parts of Roaring Run Trail and Rock Furnace Trail are handicapped accessible.

**Site Description:** The 653-acre recreation area contains deciduous, coniferous, mixed, and early successional forests, shrub/scrub, grassland/savanna, fallow fields, marsh, riparian, pond, river, stream, and reclaimed/abandoned mine land areas. There are huge rocks and waterfalls, as well as unique plants and an abundance of spring wildflowers.

**Site Information:** Free admission. Nearly 15 miles of hiking/mountain biking trails are featured within the recreation area. One trail even has a suspension bridge spanning Roaring Run. Information (including detailed maps), restrooms (some handicapped accessible), signage, picnic facilities, guided tours, environmental education programs, and custom programs are available. Mountain biking, canoeing/kayaking, and hunting occur on site. Leashed pets are permitted. Restaurants, gasoline, and convenience/grocery stores are located nearby.

**Key Birds and Wildlife:** Osprey, Bald Eagle, Great Blue Heron, Green Heron, Belted Kingfisher, Double-crested Cormorant, Rose-breasted Grosbeak, Scarlet Tanager, Red-bellied Woodpecker, Wood Thrush, American Redstart, Baltimore Oriole, Pileated Woodpecker, Gray Catbird, Cerulean Warbler, Acadian Flycatcher, Indigo Bunting, Eastern Bluebird, Tennessee Warbler, Kentucky Warbler, Turkey Vulture. White-tailed deer and black bear may be seen here. Fishing is good in the river.

**Other Comments:** This area is a fine example of the cooperation and efforts of private foundations, the state Department of Conservation and Natural Resources, and members of the local community to restore the land, repair the scars, and provide recreational opportunities for all. Some remnants of the Pennsylvania Main Line Canal can still be found today. There are also great views of the Kiski Valley. For more information and specific directions to Roaring Run, Rock Furnace, and Edmon trailheads, visit www.roaringrun.org.

**Contact Information:**
Roaring Run Watershed Association
616 1st Street Extension
P.O. Box 333
Apollo, PA 15613
(724) 478-3366

*Eastern Bluebird*

# Beaver County

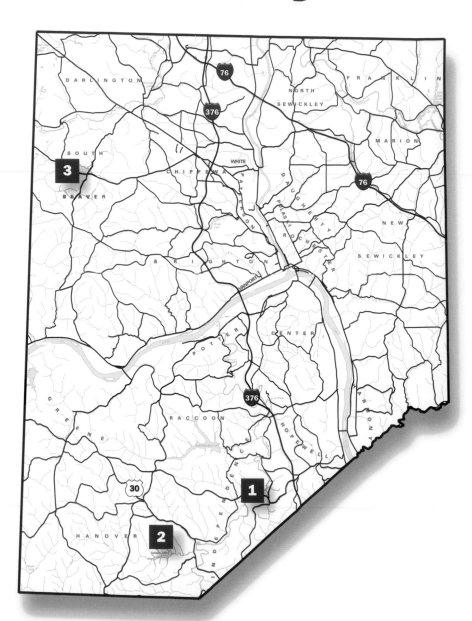

## Legend

 Handicapped Accessibility

 Hiking Trails

 Biking Trails

 Restrooms

 Dogs Allowed

# 1 INDEPENDENCE MARSH

**Location:** Independence Marsh is located in Independence Township, Beaver County, on PA-151 west of PA-60.

**Owner/Manager:** Beaver County/Beaver County Conservation District

**GPS Coordinates:** 40° 33' 3" N, 80° 19' 5" W

**Directions, Access, & Parking:** Exit PA-60/I-376 at the PA-151 exit and head west on PA-151 for 2.9 miles to Cowpath Road. Follow Cowpath Road for 0.3 miles to a green iron gate on the right, which marks the entrance to Independence Marsh.

**Site Description:** Independence Marsh features two large ponds, the larger of which attracts waterfowl in spring and fall. The smaller pond is more heavily vegetated. During summers featuring little rainfall, the smaller pond dries up completely and the larger pond develops extensive mudflats that can be good for shorebirding. However, the conditions of the mudflats are variable from year to year, and in some years both ponds remain full throughout the summer. The gate used to be locked at unpredictable times, but the report from the Beaver County Conservation District states that the gate is always open. Visitors are welcome from dawn to dusk.

**Site Information:** Free admission. There are flat trails around both of the ponds that can be leisurely hiked and birded in about one hour. Waterproof shoes are recommended for hiking, especially in spring. Features include an observation deck, observation blind, visitor center, restrooms, drinking water, and education programs. Restaurants, campgrounds, gasoline, and convenience stores are close by.

**Key Birds and Wildlife:** Breeding species include Green Heron, Willow Flycatcher, Tree Swallow, Eastern Bluebird, Yellow Warbler, Common Yellowthroat, Swamp Sparrow, and Orchard Oriole. Migrant species include Fox Sparrow, Lincoln's Sparrow, White-crowned Sparrow, shorebirds, warblers, and waterfowl. Great Egret, Marsh Wren, Northern Waterthrush, Virginia Rail, Sora, Osprey, and Bald Eagle are rare.

**Other Comments:** The sign at the entrance to the marsh reads "Beaver County Conservation District." Note that "Independence Marsh" is simply a colloquial name for the location, used by birders.

**Contact Information:**
Beaver County Conservation District
156 Cowpath Road
Aliquippa, PA 15001
(724) 378-1701

*Dunlin and other shorebirds*

# 2 RACCOON CREEK STATE PARK

**Location:** Raccoon Creek State Park is located in southern Beaver County, near Hookstown and 25 miles west of Pittsburgh.

**Owner/Manager:** Commonwealth of Pennsylvania/ Pennsylvania Department of Conservation and Natural Resources

**GPS Coordinates:** 40° 30' 14" N, 80° 25' 25" W

**Directions, Access, & Parking:** From the Pittsburgh area follow US-22/US-30 west towards Weirton. At the intersection with US-60, you will have to make a loop to the right to remain on US-22/US-30 west. When US-30 exits to the north, remain on US-22 west. Exit at the PA-18 exit toward Florence/Burgettstown, then turn left onto PA-18 north. Follow PA-18 north directly into the heart of Raccoon Creek State Park. Parking is available for cars and buses. Raccoon Creek Wildflower Reserve can be reached within the park by traveling east on Raccoon Park Road from PA-18 to US-30. If you are outside the park and to the east, follow US-30 to the reserve.

**Site Description:** The 7,323-acre Raccoon Creek State Park contains deciduous and early successional forests, cultivated fields, wetlands, lakes, and streams. The wildflower reserve on the eastern end of the park has miles of trails and provides excellent viewing of wildlife along Raccoon Creek. The park is part of Important Bird Area #13.

**Site Information:** Free admission. Hiking-only and multi-use trails, detailed wildflower and trail information, a visitor center, restrooms, drinking water, and interpretive signage are available. Boating, fishing, swimming, and horseback riding are part of the park's recreation. Hunting is permitted. Lodging, restaurants, and a campground are close by.

**Key Birds and Wildlife:** Louisiana Waterthrush, Yellow-throated Warbler, Cerulean Warbler, Northern Parula, Wood Duck, Cooper's Hawk, Chimney Swift, Ruby-throated Hummingbird, Belted Kingfisher, Northern Flicker, Least Flycatcher, Barn Swallow, Brown Creeper, Blue-gray Gnatcatcher, Hermit Thrush, Blue-winged Warbler, Scarlet Tanager, Indigo Bunting, Orchard Oriole. Wild Turkeys may be seen near camping and picnicking spots. The Wildflower Reserve has six hiking-only trails that are great for birding. The Wildflower Reserve also has a Turkey Vulture roost. Thirty-three species of warblers have been found in Raccoon Creek Valley. Mammals here include American beaver, American mink, and red fox.

**Other Comments:** The Raccoon Creek State Park Wildflower Reserve covers 314 acres and contains a diverse assortment of wildflowers. Over 700 species have been identified. The reserve is closed to all activities other than hiking on designated trails. Pets are prohibited in the reserve. The Wildflower Reserve is open 8 a.m. to sunset. Visit www.dcnr.state.pa.us/stateparks for more information.

**Contact Information:**
Raccoon Creek State Park
3000 State Route 18
Hookstown, PA 15050
(724) 899-2200

*Black-throated Green Warbler*

**3** STATE GAME LANDS 285

**Location:** State Game Lands 285 is located in Beaver County, near the town of Cannelton.

**Owner/Manager:** Commonwealth of Pennsylvania/ Pennsylvania Game Commission

**GPS Coordinates:** 40° 47' 53" N, 80° 28' 40" W (east parking lot on Cannelton Road)

**Directions, Access, & Parking:** From Beaver Falls take PA-51 north for approximately 6 miles. Turn left onto Cannelton Road to access State Game Lands 285. There is parking for 5–10 cars.

**Site Description:** The 2,839-acre State Game Lands 285 is strip-mined lands bisected by the north fork of Little Beaver Creek. It contains deciduous and mixed deciduous forests, a pine plantation, fallow and farmed fields, shrub/ scrub, grassland, and a stream.

**Site Information:** Free admission. Cannelton, Watts Mills, and Valley roads cover much of the SGL. Trails from those roads lead to a variety of habitats. Mountain biking, snowmobiling, and hunting are permitted.

**Key Birds and Wildlife:** American Woodcock, Whip-poor-will, Ruffed Grouse, Henslow's Sparrow, Grasshopper Sparrow, Savannah Sparrow, Bobolink, Eastern Meadowlark, Rough-legged Hawk, Prairie Warbler, Yellow-breasted Chat, Eastern Bluebird, Orchard Oriole.

**Other Comments:** Private properties and businesses stretch along the railroad tracks and Little Beaver Creek; it might be difficult to tell when you are in the SGL. When hiking the trails, a GPS would be helpful; the strip-mined terrain is confusing. Visit www.pgc.state.pa.us for more information.

**Contact Information:**
Pennsylvania Game Commission, Southwest Region
4820 Route 711
Bolivar, PA 15923
(724) 238-9523

Clay-colored Sparrow

# Bedford County

## Legend

 Handicapped Accessibility

 Hiking Trails

 Biking Trails

 Restrooms

 Dogs Allowed

# 1 ALLEGHENY FRONT HAWK WATCH

**Location:** Allegheny Front Hawk Watch is located on the Bedford County and Somerset County line, near Central City.

**Owner/Manager:** Allegheny Plateau Audubon Society

**GPS Coordinates:** 40° 4' 54" N, 78° 43' 43" W

**Directions, Access, & Parking:** From US-30 at Reels Corners, take PA-160 north for 4 miles into Central City, passing Thunder Valley Raceway on the left. Entering Central City, PA-160 north makes a sharp right at a BP gas station. When PA-160 north makes a sharp left, instead go straight onto Lambert Street (SR1018). Go slowly and watch for the "rough" railroad crossing. After the railroad crossing bear to the right to stay on Lambert Street. Lambert Street becomes Shaffer Mountain Road (SR1018) outside Central City. Proceed 1.4 miles out of Central City and bear right at a Y-intersection onto Lambert Mountain Road (SR1035). On Lambert Mountain Road, go 2.9 miles through State Game Lands 228 to a small four-way intersection with Fleegle Road. Go straight through the intersection staying on Lambert Mountain Road. The Daley Cemetery will be on the right; this will become a gravel road. Go 0.5 miles to a blue gate on the right. Turn right at the blue gate and go 0.25 miles to the Hawk Watch parking area. There are aluminum falcon symbols along either side of this dirt road. If the gate is closed, find a place to park near the gate and walk the 0.25 miles to the watch site. Buses can only go as far as the blue gate. Beyond the gate there is access for cars and vans, with parking for more than 10 cars. Handicapped parking is available at the watch site on top of the mountain. It is recommended that you follow the roads listed here rather than using an alternate route chosen by your GPS; some roads in these mountains can be gravel, poorly maintained, winding, steep, and only suitable for four-wheel drive vehicles.

**Site Description:** Located on five acres, the Allegheny Front Hawk Watch is the eastern edge of the Allegheny Plateau at an elevation of 2,850 feet. It sits approximately 800 feet above a valley and gives a nearly 180-degree view. On a clear day one can see as far north as Blue Knob, as far south as I-70, and as far east as the ridges beyond Tussey Mountain. This site provides a unique vantage point since most high mountain views in Pennsylvania are heavily wooded and inaccessible. Allegheny Front Hawk Watch has been designated as Important Bird Area #84.

**Site Information:** Free admission. A portable (handicapped accessible) restroom is available. This is a private reserve with environmental education programs. Restaurants and convenience/grocery stores are located in Central City.

**Key Birds and Wildlife:** Golden Eagle, Osprey, Bald Eagle, Northern Harrier, Sharp-shinned Hawk, Cooper's Hawk, Red-shouldered Hawk, Broad-winged Hawk, Red-tailed Hawk, American Kestrel, Northern Goshawk, Rough-legged Hawk, Merlin, Peregrine Falcon. Small birds and an occasional rarity can be seen flying past the watch site or landing on the mountain.

**Other Comments:** The site is open from 9 a.m. to 5 p.m. daily, weather permitting. Birds do not fly if it is raining, so the Hawk Watch might be closed for the day. Counters from the Allegheny Plateau Audubon Society staff the site from February through May and August through December, seven days a week. The road, after passing through the gate, is not maintained between December and February. Winds from the east will push the birds closer to the plateau for more spectacular viewing. Fog can obscure the view, and temperatures and winds can be uncomfortable. Bring extra layers of clothing, a chair or blanket for seating, and water and snacks if you plan to stay for several hours. Visit www.alleghenyplateauaudubon.org for more information.

**Contact Information:**
Allegheny Plateau Audubon Society
257 Kring Street
Johnstown, PA 15904

*Golden Eagle*

# 2 DUNNINGS CREEK WETLANDS

**Location:** Dunnings Creek Wetlands is located in Bedford County, near the town of Pleasantville.

**Owner/Manager:** Private

**GPS Coordinates:** 40° 9' 25" N, 78° 36' 49" W

**Directions, Access, & Parking:** From Johnstown take PA-56 east through Windber and through the town of Pleasantville. Turn right onto Dunnings Creek Road, then turn right on Mennonite Road. This is a farm lane that goes directly to Dunnings Creek Wetlands and Whitetail Wetlands. Park in the circle to the right of the white farmhouse to meet your guide. There is parking for 5–10 cars. Handicapped access has not yet been developed to the wetlands. For directions from I-76/Pennsylvania Turnpike, see Whitetail Wetlands.

**Site Description:** The 100-acre Dunnings Creek Wetlands contains deciduous forest, grassland/savanna, fallow fields, and wetlands areas. It is managed for waterfowl, shorebirds, reptiles, and amphibians. Sixty-five acres of uplands have been planted with corn, millet, partridge pea, switch grass, and sunflowers to encourage wildlife. A five-acre area contains alders for management of woodcocks. The remaining fields are managed for butterflies and songbirds.

**Site Information:** Guides and helpers are provided to lead activities, presentations, discussions, and walks along the trails. Restaurants, camping, lodging, and convenience/grocery stores are located nearby.

**Key Birds and Wildlife:** Wood Duck, Hooded Merganser, Blue-winged Teal, Great Egret, American Kestrel, Virginia Rail, Sora, Black-billed Cuckoo, Yellow-billed Cuckoo, Spotted Sandpiper, Common Snipe, Ring-necked Pheasant, Ruffed Grouse, Wild Turkey, Northern Bobwhite, American Woodcock, Great Horned Owl, Barn Owl, Barred Owl, Red-headed Woodpecker, Pileated Woodpecker, Marsh Wren, Sedge Wren, Golden-winged Warbler, Northern Waterthrush, Vesper Sparrow, Grasshopper Sparrow, Henslow's Sparrow, Bobolink, Orchard Oriole, Purple Finch, Pine Siskin. Other bird species such as Northern Rough-winged Swallow, Tree Swallow, Purple Martin, and Cedar Waxwing have used the wetlands for hunting insects. Over 18 species of fish live in the Dunnings Creek Wetlands, attracting Bald Eagle, Osprey, and Belted Kingfisher during migration. The area is also home to caddisflies, mayflies, dragonflies, damselflies, and aquatic beetles. This insect population has attracted bats that are encouraged to nest in bat boxes. Muskrat, American mink, American beaver, coyote, and even northern river otter are also found here.

**Other Comments:** Wetlands are wet, so dress accordingly. Dunnings Creek Wetlands is a private reserve, open to the public only by reservations with at least one month's advance notice; call (814) 754-5727. This sanctuary was created in cooperation with the United States Fish and Wildlife Service's "Partners for Fish and Wildlife Program." Visit www.alleghenyplateauaudubon.org for more information.

**Contact Information:**
Dr. Tom Dick
(814) 754-5727

Great Egret

Northern Shoveler

## 3 SHAWNEE STATE PARK

**Location:** Shawnee State Park is located in Bedford County, near the town of Bedford.

**Owner/Manager:** Commonwealth of Pennsylvania/ Pennsylvania Department of Conservation and Natural Resources

**GPS Coordinates:** 40° 1' 33" N, 78° 38' 7" W

**Directions, Access, & Parking:** Located at 132 State Park Road, access to Shawnee State Park is just east of Schellsburg, along US-30 and about 10 miles west of the Bedford exit of I-76/Pennsylvania Turnpike. The park is also easily accessed from the south via PA-31 and PA-96 (Shawnee Road). There is easy access and parking for cars, and the park is handicapped accessible.

**Site Description:** The 3,983-acre Shawnee State Park is home to 451-acre Shawnee Lake. The park contains deciduous and mixed forests, a lake, a sand and turf beach, and little open area. The wooded hills and valleys of the park are surrounded by large farm fields.

**Site Information:** Free admission. Visitors can walk remnants of the historic Forbes Trail in the park. On-site trails, information, restrooms, drinking water, picnic pavilions, vending machines, camping, guided tours, and environmental education programs are available. Mountain biking, motor boating (electric only), canoeing/kayaking, snowmobiling, swimming, fishing and ice fishing, and hunting are permitted. Camping facilities are in the park. Restaurants, lodging, gasoline, and convenience/grocery stores are located nearby.

**Key Birds and Wildlife:** Wood Duck, Green Heron, Ruffed Grouse, Pine Warbler, Worm-eating Warbler, Blue-winged Warbler, Golden-winged Warbler, Winter Wren, Golden Eagle, Bald Eagle, Greater White-fronted Goose, Black-legged Kittiwake, Black Skimmer, White Ibis. Spring and fall waterfowl migrations can be great. Large weather systems bring waterfowl fallouts to Shawnee. Hundreds of Common Loons and Long-tailed Ducks have appeared in the spring. Many locations around the lake provide easy viewing. The beach area at Shawnee has had Piping Plover and Sanderling in the past. Largemouth and smallmouth bass, northern pike, walleye, and muskie can be found in the lake.

**Other Comments:** The park is named for American Indians who lived in the vicinity of the park in the early 1700s during their westward migration. General John Forbes camped his army within the park boundaries in 1758 while building the Forbes Road, a wagon-wide swath through Pennsylvania. The road was instrumental in the English campaign against the French at Fort Duquesne, Pittsburgh.
Visit www.dcnr.state.pa.us/stateparks for more information.

**Contact Information:**
Shawnee State Park
132 State Park Road
Schellsburg, PA 15559
(814) 733-4218

Bonaparte's Gull

Ring-necked Duck

# Butler County

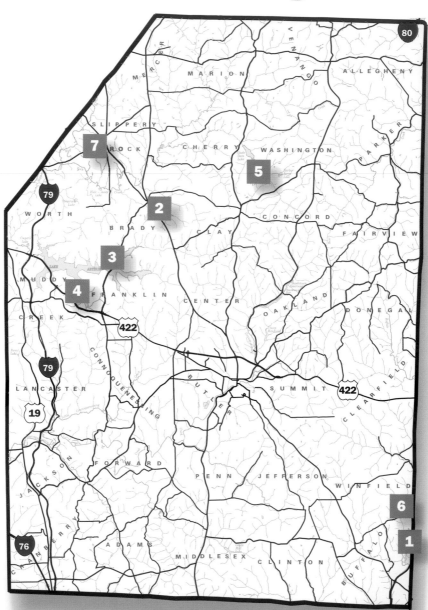

## Legend

 Handicapped Accessibility

 Hiking Trails

 Biking Trails

 Restrooms

 Dogs Allowed

## 1 BUFFALO CREEK VALLEY AND BUTLER-FREEPORT COMMUNITY TRAIL

**Location:** Buffalo Creek Valley is located in southeastern Butler County and neighboring western Armstrong County. It spreads along several creeks and runs from Freeport in the south to north of State Game Lands 164, 259, and 304. The Butler-Freeport Community Trail, which runs over 20 miles from Freeport to the City of Butler, provides easy access to the southern third of the Buffalo Creek Valley.

**Owner/Manager:** Buffalo Creek Valley encompasses many jurisdictions. The trail is managed by the Butler-Freeport Community Trail Council, Inc.

**GPS Coordinates:** 40° 43' 45" N, 79° 44' 50" W

**Directions, Access, & Parking:** From Pittsburgh take PA-28 north to Exit 17 (PA-356/Butler/Freeport). At the end of the ramp, turn right on PA-356 and travel 3.6 miles. Turn right onto Sarver Road (SR2018) and drive 0.5 miles. After crossing a creek, turn left into the bike-trail parking area located at 570 Sarver Road. Parking is available for 5–10 cars and the site is handicapped accessible.

**Site Description:** The Butler-Freeport Trail is located in the southern portion of the 60,000-acre Buffalo Creek Valley. The valley consists of deciduous, mixed, and early successional forests, as well as grassland/savanna and stream areas. Of special conservation interest is the unfragmented forest and riparian habitat. Much of the Butler-Freeport Trail meanders through a steep-walled valley dominated by eastern hemlock and birch. The trail side also boasts a high diversity of wildflowers in spring and late summer. Buffalo Creek Valley has been designated as Important Bird Area #22.

**Site Information:** Free admission. The trail has restrooms (May–October), benches, and tables. Mountain biking, horseback riding, cross-country skiing, and leashed pets are permitted. Lodging, restaurants, gasoline, and convenience stores are close by.

**Key Birds and Wildlife:** Breeding birds include Common Merganser, Wood Duck, Louisiana Waterthrush, Yellow-throated Warbler, Kentucky Warbler, Worm-eating Warbler, Hooded Warbler, Yellow-throated Vireo, Acadian Flycatcher. Spring and fall migration can be dramatic at this site with 20 species of warblers expected. Reports of Bald Eagle are becoming common.

**Other Comments:** Caution should be used during hunting season. The Butler-Freeport Trail preserves the route taken by Butler County's first railroad in 1871. Visiting the southern portion of the trail puts you within minutes of Todd Nature Reserve. Visit www.butlerfreeporttrail.org for more information.

**Contact Information:**
Butler-Freeport Community Trail Council, Inc.
P.O. Box 533
Saxonburg, PA 16056
(724) 352-4783

Cerulean Warbler

*Grasshopper Sparrow*

## 2 JENNINGS ENVIRONMENTAL EDUCATION CENTER

**Location:** Jennings Environmental Education Center is located in Butler County, near the town of Slippery Rock.

**Owner/Manager:** Commonwealth of Pennsylvania/ Pennsylvania Department of Conservation and Natural Resources

**GPS Coordinates:** 41° 0' 3" N, 80° 0' 9" W

**Directions, Access, & Parking:** From Pittsburgh take PA-8/William Flynn Highway north for approximately 40 miles. Turn left (south) onto PA-528/Prospect Road and watch for signs. Parking is available for cars and buses. The site is handicapped accessible.

**Site Description:** The 300-acre Jennings Environmental Center is home to deciduous and early successional forests, shrub/scrub, grassland/savanna, marsh, and stream areas. The site boasts a 20-acre relict prairie, which is in full bloom in late July and early August. It provides a habitat for plants that are unique to a prairie. Shelf fungi and morels also can be found here. Jennings Environmental Center is part of Important Bird Area #12.

**Site Information:** Free admission. Thirteen woodland trails, information, a visitor center with exhibits and displays, restrooms, drinking water, interpretive signs, and guided tours are available. Programs and workshops are offered to students, teachers, civic groups, and the community on a variety of environmental concerns. Lodging, restaurants, gasoline, and convenience stores are located nearby.

**Key Birds and Wildlife:** Barred Owl, Indigo Bunting, Hooded Warbler, Blue-winged Warbler, Ovenbird, Cerulean Warbler, Scarlet Tanager, and Field Sparrow. The endangered massasauga rattlesnake is a prairie inhabitant. Bog lemming, least weasel, red eft, and viceroy butterfly may be seen along a trail.

**Other Comments:** Jennings Environmental Education Center was named after Dr. Otto Emery Jennings, a renowned botanist, and was the first reserve in Pennsylvania established to protect a single species of plant, the blazing star. Jennings, known as O. E., taught that "the highest use of a piece of land may be nonuse." The grounds are open 8 a.m. to sunset, seven days a week. Visit www.dcnr.state.pa.us/stateparks for more information.

**Contact Information:**
Jennings Environmental Education Center
2951 Prospect Road
Slippery Rock, PA 16057-5023
(724) 794-6011

*White-throated Sparrow*

## 3 MORAINE STATE PARK: ROUTE 528 BOAT LAUNCH
### (AND VICINITY)

**Location:** Moraine State Park's Route 528 Boat Launch is in Butler County, near West Liberty Boro.

**Owner/Manager:** Commonwealth of Pennsylvania/Pennsylvania Department of Conservation and Natural Resources

**GPS Coordinates:** 40° 57' 7" N, 80° 2' 28" W

**Directions, Access, & Parking:** From Pittsburgh take I-79 N to Exit 99 (US-422). Follow US-422 east for 5.8 miles to the PA-528 (Prospect) exit. At the end of the ramp, turn left onto PA-528. Cross over US-422 and drive another 1.3 miles. Cross a large bridge and immediately make a sharp right turn to go under the bridge to the parking lot and boat ramp. Parking is available for cars and buses. Parts of the park are handicapped accessible, but restrooms here are not. Continue north in the state park along PA-528; the next right turn leads to the Upper 528 Boat Launch and opportunities to view Muddy Creek. Go a few feet farther on PA-528, and you can pull off on the left to hike part of the North Country Trail. Continue a short distance on PA-528 and make a right turn onto Barkley Road; look and listen for passerines. At the end of this road, you will find a parking lot, a Mine Treatment Exhibit, and another opportunity to look for waterfowl in Muddy Creek.

**Site Description:** Moraine State Park's Route 528 Boat Launch region contains deciduous and early successional forests, shrub/scrub, swamp, marsh, a 3,225-acre lake, and stream areas. Moraine State Park is part of Important Bird Area #12.

**Site Information:** Free admission. On-site trails, information, restrooms, interpretive signage, and drinking water. Hunting is permitted, and mountain biking, motorized boating, and canoeing/kayaking are allowed in the park. Lodging, restaurants, campground, gasoline, and convenience stores are close by.

**Key Birds and Wildlife:** Hooded Merganser, Great Blue Heron, Green Heron, American Woodcock, Yellow-billed Cuckoo. Northern Flicker, Great Crested Flycatcher, Red-eyed Vireo, Brown Creeper, Golden-crowned Kinglet, Blue-gray Gnatcatcher, Prairie Warbler, Scarlet Tanager, Swamp Sparrow, Indigo Bunting, Brown-headed Cowbird, Baltimore Oriole. A Cliff Swallow colony is visible at the boat launch under the PA-528 bridge. The park is a popular stop-off for migrating ducks and geese. Osprey and Bald Eagle nest here, and occasionally rails and American Bitterns may be seen.

**Other Comments:** A volunteer organization that supports Moraine State Park is the Moraine Preservation Fund. It has been instrumental in the Osprey and Barn Owl Reintroduction Programs, wildlife education classes, a Native Plant & Butterfly Trail, a gift shop and nature center at McDaniel's Boat Launch, and a pontoon boat offering interpretive boat tours on Lake Arthur. Visit www.dcnr.state.pa.us/stateparks or www.morainepreservationfund.com for more information.

**Contact Information:**
Moraine State Park
225 Pleasant Valley Road
Portersville, PA 16051
(724) 368-8811

Moraine Preservation Fund
118 North Shore Drive
Portersville, PA 16051
(724) 368-9500

*Baltimore Oriole*

# 4 MORAINE STATE PARK: SOUTH SHORE

**Location:** Moraine State Park's South Shore is located in Butler County, near Portersville.

**Owner/Manager:** Commonwealth of Pennsylvania/ Pennsylvania Department of Conservation and Natural Resources

**GPS Coordinates:** 40° 56' 26" N, 80° 5' 55" W

**Directions, Access, & Parking:** From Pittsburgh take I-79 N to Exit 99 (US-422). Follow US-422 east for 2.4 miles to the Moraine State Park exit. At the end of the ramp, turn left onto Pleasant Valley Road and drive 0.5 miles to the park office on the left. Parts of the park are handicapped accessible. Parking is available for cars and buses. From the park office, follow the driving loop around Pleasant Valley. Stop at the numerous parking areas that overlook the lake. From the first boat launch parking lot, walk the Sunken Garden Trail through a marshy area. Continue viewing the lake and stopping along the way. Windy Knob, on your right, can be a good place to walk. Take the Bear Run turn to the right for one more view of the lake. Drive farther on the loop to return to the park office. Turn right on Pleasant Valley Road, cross under the highway, and turn left to go east on US-422. Exit at PA-528. At the end of the ramp, turn left to cross over the highway and pass its other exit ramp. Immediately turn left onto Old US-422. Spend some time at the Waterfowl Observation Area platform and also drive to the end of the road. Here you can view Muskrat and Beaver Coves and walk Wyggeston Trail.

**Site Description:** Moraine State Park's South Shore contains deciduous and early successional forests, shrub/ scrub, grassland/savanna, marsh, the 3,225-acre Lake Arthur, and stream areas. Moraine State Park is part of Important Bird Area #12.

**Site Information:** Free admission. Numerous hiking trails, a biking trail, a mountain biking trail, information, restrooms, and drinking water are available. Motorized boating (up to 20 hp), canoeing/kayaking, fishing, and hunting are allowed in the park. The state park has camping areas and cabin rentals. Lodging, restaurants, gasoline, and convenience stores are close by.

**Key Birds and Wildlife:** Bald Eagle, Osprey, Hooded Merganser, Common Loon, Snow Goose, Great Blue Heron, Green Heron, Virginia Rail, Sora, Ring-billed Gull, Great Horned Owl, Alder Flycatcher, Blue-headed Vireo, Tree Swallow, White-breasted Nuthatch, Blue-gray Gnatcatcher, Chestnut-sided Warbler, Black-throated Green Warbler, Ovenbird, Yellow-breasted Chat, Swamp Sparrow, White-crowned Sparrow, Indigo Bunting, Orchard Oriole, Baltimore Oriole. This is an excellent area for fall waterfowl migration. On occasion, Northern Shrike, Snow Bunting, Purple Finch, or American Pipit may be found. Rarities such as Black-headed Gull, Red-throated Loon, White-winged Scoter, and Red Phalarope have been found within the park.

**Other Comments:** The rolling hills are reminders of the moraines left behind when glaciers melted away during the last glacial period, but the 16,725-acre park is an outstanding achievement of environmental engineering. Scars from coal mining and oil and gas drilling were sealed and covered. Muddy Creek was dammed in 1968 and Lake Arthur was formed. By 1970 the lake had filled and Moraine State Park was founded. Visit www.dcnr.state.pa.us/stateparks or www.morainepreservationfund.com for more information.

**Contact Information:**
Moraine State Park
225 Pleasant Valley Road
Portersville, PA 16051
(724) 368-8811

Moraine Preservation Fund
118 North Shore Drive
Portersville, PA 16051
(724) 368-9500

## 5 STATE GAME LANDS 095
## HILLIARDS
### (ALSO KNOWN AS THE GLADES)

**Location:** State Game Lands 095 is located in Butler County, near the town of Hilliards.

**Owner/Manager:** Commonwealth of Pennsylvania/ Pennsylvania Game Commission

**GPS Coordinates:** 41° 3' 4" N, 79° 53' 14" W

**Directions, Access, & Parking:** From Butler take US-422 west. Turn onto PA-8 north, then onto PA-308 north towards Moniteau. Just before the town of Moniteau, turn right onto Tinker Road and follow it to the parking area at the lake. There is easy access and available parking for cars.

**Site Description:** This area of State Game Lands 095 contains several large ponds, marsh, dead-tree swamp, and abandoned field areas. The surrounding acreage contains deciduous and early successional forests, marsh, shrub/ scrub, hemlock stands, and stream areas. This area has been designated as Important Bird Area #11.

**Site Information:** Free admission for day use only. The North Country Trail runs north–south through the site, staying west of the lake. There are a number of roads that are closed to unauthorized vehicles but excellent for walking and seeing birds and other wildlife. Hunting is permitted.

**Key Birds and Wildlife:** Wood Duck, Green Heron, Osprey, Bald Eagle, American Kestrel, Virginia Rail, Sora, Common Moorhen, American Coot, Chimney Swift, Belted Kingfisher, Eastern Wood-Pewee, Willow Flycatcher, Red-eyed Vireo, Northern Rough-winged Swallow, Veery, Cedar Waxwing, Chestnut-sided Warbler, Black-throated Green Warbler, Scarlet Tanager, Rusty Blackbird, Indigo Bunting, Eastern Meadowlark. During the 2nd Pennsylvania Breeding Bird Atlas project, 86 species were recorded here.

**Other Comments:** The PGC propagation area at the north end of Glade Dam Lake is strictly off limits to birders and hunters. Be aware that deer flies, deer ticks, and poison ivy can be problems. Visit www.pgc.state.pa.us for more information.

**Contact Information:**
Pennsylvania Game Commission, Northwest Region
P.O. Box 31
Franklin, PA 16323
(814) 432-3187

Ross's Goose

# 6 TODD NATURE RESERVE

## (FORMERLY TODD SANCTUARY)

**Location:** Todd Nature Reserve is located in Butler County, near the town of Sarver.

**Owner/Manager:** Audubon Society of Western Pennsylvania

**GPS Coordinates:** 40° 43' 59" N, 79° 42' 9" W

**Directions, Access, & Parking:** From Pittsburgh take PA-28 north to Exit 17 (PA-356/Butler/Freeport). At the end of the ramp, head north on PA-356 for 0.8 miles. Turn right onto Monroe Road and follow it for 1.2 miles to a fork in the road, bearing right onto Kepple Road past Buffalo Golf Course. After 1.8 miles, the reserve is marked by a sign on the right. Parking is available for cars.

**Site Description:** The 220-acre Todd Nature Reserve contains deciduous, coniferous, and mixed forests, a pond, and rocky and pristine streams. The reserve is wooded, with a significant area comprised of hemlock forest. Todd Nature Reserve is part of the Buffalo Creek Valley Important Bird Area #22.

**Site Information:** Free admission. The nature reserve and its trails are open for day use only. Trail maps and information are available at the cabin, a short walk from the parking lot. A naturalist is on site during summer months. The nature reserve has no public restrooms; a portable restroom is available during the summer. Restaurants, gasoline, and convenience stores are close by.

**Key Birds and Wildlife:** Red-tailed Hawk, Red-shouldered Hawk, Cooper's Hawk, Barred Owl, Yellow-billed Cuckoo, Chimney Swift, Belted Kingfisher, Red-bellied Woodpecker, Hairy Woodpecker, Pileated Woodpecker, Eastern Wood-Pewee, Acadian Flycatcher, Wood Thrush, Ovenbird, Louisiana Waterthrush, American Redstart, Kentucky Warbler, Hooded Warbler, Black-throated Green Warbler, Scarlet Tanager, Indigo Bunting. Black bear, white-tailed deer, and coyote may be seen. The reserve's streams support a wide variety of salamanders.

**Other Comments:** Todd Nature Reserve is closed during the regular deer hunting season, generally two weeks following Thanksgiving. Visit www.aswp.org for more information.

**Contact Information:**
Audubon Society of Western Pennsylvania
614 Dorseyville Road
Pittsburgh, PA 15238
(412) 963-6100

*Eastern Screech-Owl*

## 7 WOLF CREEK NARROWS

**Location:** Wolf Creek Narrows is located in Butler County, near the town of Slippery Rock.

**Owner/Manager:** Western Pennsylvania Conservancy

**GPS Coordinates:** 41° 3' 51" N, 80° 5' 14" W

**Directions, Access, & Parking:** From the Slippery Rock exit of I-79, proceed east on PA-108 to the town of Slippery Rock. At the traffic light in the center of town, turn left on PA-258, go one block, and turn left onto Water Street. Follow it for approximately 2 miles until the road crosses Wolf Creek. Cross the bridge and look for a small parking area at the head of a dirt lane on the left. Do not block the lane, but park on the left side toward the creek. Walk back across the bridge. The trailhead is on the left side of the road. Look for a large sign and a bulletin board. Parking is available for cars.

**Site Description:** The 100-acre Wolf Creek Narrows is home to mixed forest and stream areas. This site contains Wolf Creek, a beautiful stream surrounded by a forest of hardwoods and hemlocks. It is known for its spring wildflowers, and there are also several uncommon plants that grow in this area.

**Site Information:** Free admission. On-site trails and interpretive signs are available. Canoeing and kayaking are permitted. Lodging, restaurants, gasoline, and convenience stores are located nearby.

**Key Birds and Wildlife:** Wild Turkey, Ruffed Grouse, Spotted Sandpiper, and Cerulean Warbler are seen regularly here. The 2nd Pennsylvania Breeding Bird Atlas lists 99 species of birds at this site, including 14 species of warblers.

**Other Comments:** The steep, narrow valley with 50-foot cliffs on either side may have been formed when melting glaciers eroded the ceiling of a cave. Visit www.paconserve.org for more information.

**Contact Information:**
Western Pennsylvania Conservancy
800 Waterfront Drive
Pittsburgh, PA 15222
(412) 288-2777

Indigo Bunting

# Clarion County

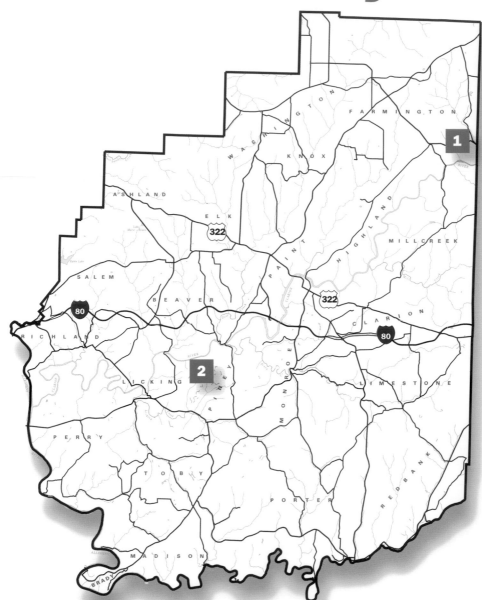

## Legend

 Handicapped Accessibility

 Hiking Trails

 Biking Trails

 Restrooms

 Dogs Allowed

## 1 COOK FOREST STATE PARK

**Location:** Cook Forest State Park straddles the boundaries of Clarion, Forest, and Jefferson counties, near the town of Cooksburg.

**Owner/Manager:** Commonwealth of Pennsylvania/ Pennsylvania Department of Conservation and Natural Resources

**GPS Coordinates:** 41° 19' 55" N, 79° 12' 28" W (park office)

**Directions, Access, & Parking:** From Pittsburgh: take I-79 N to I-80 E. Go east to Exit 60/Shippenville. Take PA-66 north toward Marienville. At the intersection of PA-66 and PA-36 in the village of Leeper, turn right (south) onto PA-36. Follow PA-36 into Cook Forest. Just before you cross the bridge over the Clarion River, turn left onto River Road. The park office is 100 yards down River Road on the left side. From the east: follow I-80 W to Exit 78. Follow PA-36 north into the park. Parking is available for cars and buses. Many facilities and attractions are handicapped accessible.

**Site Description:** The 8,500-acre Cook Forest State Park is home to deciduous, coniferous, and mixed forests, river, and stream areas. The site is recognized for its towering, old-growth eastern hemlock and white pine. The "Forest Cathedral" is a National Natural Landmark where some trees are over 150 feet tall. Two scenic views in the southeastern corner of the park are the Seneca Point Overlook and Fire Tower #9. On a clear day, you can see 15–20 miles from the 80-foot tower. Cook Forest has been designated as Important Bird Area #19.

**Site Information:** Free admission. Twenty-seven miles of trails, including parts of the Baker Trail and the Rachel Carson Trail, meander through the rolling hills and under the majestic forest canopy. Information, restrooms, drinking water, interpretive signage, and guided tours are available. Horseback riding, mountain biking, motorized boating, canoeing/kayaking, snowmobiling, ice-skating, fishing, hunting, and picnicking are permitted. Lodging, restaurants, and convenience stores are nearby. There are camping facilities in the park.

**Key Birds and Wildlife:** Bald Eagle, Least Flycatcher, Blue-headed Vireo, Cliff Swallow, Red-breasted Nuthatch, Winter Wren, Golden-crowned Kinglet, Hermit Thrush, Golden-winged Warbler, Nashville Warbler, Northern Parula, Magnolia Warbler, Pine Siskin, Blackburnian Warbler, Ruffed Grouse, Wild Turkey. This is a good site for winter finches during invasion years. Seventy-six species of birds were reported here during the Second Pennsylvania Breeding Bird Atlas project. White-tailed deer and black bear may be seen.

**Other Comments:** John Cook arrived in the area in 1826 and settled there with his wife and ten children in 1828. One hundred years later, 3,000 acres of timber that the Cook family had not logged were preserved as the beginning of the state park. Visit www.dcnr.state.pa.us/stateparks for more information.

**Contact Information:**
Cook Forest State Park
P.O. Box 120
Cooksburg, PA 16217-0120
(814) 744-8407

*Rough-legged Hawk*

# 2 PINEY TRACT STATE 🚶🚴🐕 GAME LANDS 330 (PART IS ALSO KNOWN AS MT. AIRY GRASSLANDS)

**Location:** Piney Tract State Game Lands 330 is in Clarion County, near the town of Clarion.

**Owner/Manager:** Commonwealth of Pennsylvania/Pennsylvania Game Commission

**GPS Coordinates:** 41° 8' 41" N, 79° 30' 19" W (Elliot Road at Mt. Zion Road)

**Directions, Access, & Parking:** Take I-80 to Exit 53 (Knox) and go south on Canoe Ripple Road/T385. Before you get to the river, there is a sharp right curve with a smaller road going straight; stay right on Canoe Ripple Road/SR3007. Cross the Clarion River and make the first left onto Elliot Road/T425 (at the crest of a hill). Elliot Road becomes a dirt road. Follow it for 1 mile, until you reach the crest of a hill from which you can see the expanse of grassland (SGL 330) ahead. Begin birding about 100 yards before the end of Elliot Road. Then continue a short distance to the T onto Mt. Zion Road; turn left (east) and continue 0.25 miles to a parking area on the left (look for a brochure at the parking lot). There is access for up to five cars.

**Site Description:** The 2,000-acre Piney Tract contains coniferous forest, shrub/scrub, and grassland/savanna areas and has smaller areas of deciduous forest, ponds, and wetlands. Grassland hilltops are broken up by brushy and forested streams. Acid mine drainage is being addressed. This area has been designated as Important Birding Area #21.

**Site Information:** Free admission. Several roads and hiking trails crisscross the game lands, and on-site information is available. Hunting is permitted. Gasoline, lodging, and restaurants are located nearby.

**Key Birds and Wildlife:** Upland Sandpiper, Vesper Sparrow, Henslow's Sparrow, Field Sparrow, Clay-colored Sparrow, Savannah Sparrow, Grasshopper Sparrow, Short-eared Owl, Long-eared Owl, Wood Duck, Ring-necked Pheasant, American Woodcock, Northern Shrike, Northern Harrier, Eastern Meadowlark, Horned Lark, Snow Bunting, Bobolink, Indigo Bunting, Prairie Warbler, Yellow Warbler, Yellow-breasted Chat, Dickcissel, Eastern Bluebird.

**Other Comments:** Piney Tract is an area of reclaimed strip mines that has been revegetated. Visit www.senecarocksaudubon.org for detailed directions about where to "Go Birding!" or www.pgc.state.pa.us for more information.

**Contact Information:**
Pennsylvania Game Commission, Northwest Region
P.O. Box 31
Franklin, PA 16323
(814) 432-3187

*Prairie Warbler*

# Crawford County

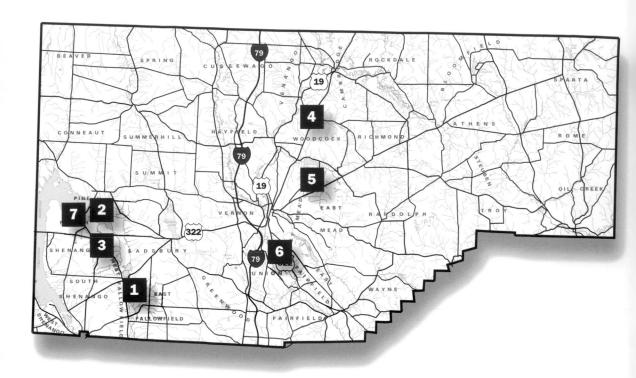

## Legend

 Handicapped Accessibility

 Hiking Trails

 Biking Trails

 Restrooms

 Dogs Allowed

# 1 HARTSTOWN MARSH – STATE GAME LANDS 214

**Location:** Hartstown Marsh is located in Crawford County, near the town of Hartstown and Pymatuning State Park.

**Owner/Manager:** Commonwealth of Pennsylvania/ Pennsylvania Game Commission

**GPS Coordinates:** 41° 33' 14" N, 80° 22' 38" W

**Directions, Access, & Parking:** From the Borough of Greenville in northwestern Mercer County, drive north on PA-18 (Conneaut Lake Road). Follow PA-18 north to the town of Hartstown. At the intersection of PA-18 and US-322, turn right to continue on PA-18 for 0.25 miles. Turn right onto Cemetery Road, follow it in a circle to head north on an unnamed gravel State Game Lands road along the marsh; the marsh will be on your right. Follow the gravel road to the parking area. There is access and parking for less than five cars.

**Site Description:** Hartstown Marsh contains deciduous and early successional forests, marsh, and riparian areas. Birding is best starting along the gravel road and parking area, and along the gravel road beyond a gate. Deciduous woodlands line the road and adjacent railroad. State Game Lands 214 is part of Important Bird Area #3.

**Site Information:** Free admission. Mountain biking, canoeing/kayaking, and hunting are permitted. A railroad service entrance is gated. Do not block the gate. Gasoline and restaurants are located nearby.

**Key Birds and Wildlife:** Common Snipe, American Coot, Bald Eagle, Common Moorhen, Warbling Vireo, Yellow-throated Vireo, Willow Flycatcher, Alder Flycatcher, Yellow Warbler, Black-throated Green Warbler, Red-winged Blackbird. Rusty Blackbird can often be found during fall migration. A Black Tern population has been present but in decreasing numbers.

**Other Comments:** The gravel/dirt road leading to this site can be rough and may contain puddles after a rain. It should probably not be attempted after a heavy rain or in a vehicle with low clearance. Drive carefully. Visit www.pgc.state.pa.us/pgc for more information.

**Contact Information:**
PA Game Commission, Northwest Region
P.O. Box 31
Franklin, PA 16323
(814) 432-3187

*Short-billed Dowitcher*

*American Coot*

# 2 LINESVILLE STATE FISH HATCHERY

**Location:** Linesville State Fish Hatchery is located in Crawford County, near the town of Linesville and surrounded by Pymatuning State Park.

**Owner/Manager:** Commonwealth of Pennsylvania/ Pennsylvania Fish and Boat Commission

**GPS Coordinates:** 41° 38' 48" N, 80° 25' 41" W

**Directions, Access, & Parking:** From Conneaut Lake follow PA-285 W approximately 6 miles to the intersection with Hartstown Road. Turn right onto Hartstown Road and continue 3.5 miles to the Linesville Hatchery on the right. There is easy access for cars and buses with parking for more than 10 cars. The site is handicapped accessible.

**Site Description:** Located on 97 developed acres (2,500 total acres), Linesville State Fish Hatchery contains deciduous and coniferous forests, marsh, lake, and pond areas. There is also a live aquarium display containing Pennsylvania native fish. This area is part of Important Bird Area #3.

**Site Information:** Free admission. Information, a visitor center, restrooms, and drinking water are available. This tract is a wildlife propagation area and is open for wildlife viewing only. Guided tours of the culture station are available on Wednesdays through Sundays from the end of March through mid-October; call the hatchery for details. Restaurants, gasoline, and convenience/grocery stores are located nearby.

**Key Birds and Wildlife:** Bald Eagle, Common Merganser, Red-breasted Merganser, Green-winged Teal, Blue-winged Teal, Great Egret, Bonaparte's Gull, Tundra Swan, Pied-billed Grebe, Horned Grebe, Red-tailed Hawk, Rough-legged Hawk, American Black Duck, Wood Duck, Northern Shoveler, American Wigeon, Eastern Bluebird, Yellow Warbler, Tree Swallow, Double-crested Cormorant, Ring-billed Gull, Turkey Vulture, Yellow-rumped Warbler, Lesser Yellowlegs, Greater Yellowlegs, Dunlin. The ponds at the hatchery entrance provide good habitat for shorebirds when they are drawn down. Cliff Swallows build nests under the eaves of the hatchery building.

**Other Comments:** Nearby Pymatuning State Park provides opportunities for camping, swimming, picnicking, canoeing/kayaking, motor boating up to 10 hp, fishing, hunting, cross-country skiing, and snowmobiling; but none of these activities are permitted at Linesville State Fish Hatchery. Other birding sites close by include the Wildlife Learning Center and State Game Lands 214. Visit www.fish.state.pa.us/images/fisheries/fcs/linesville/fcs.htm for more information.

**Contact Information:**
Linesville State Fish Hatchery
13300 Hartstown Road
Linesville, PA 16424
(814) 683-4451

Bald Eagle

## 3 MILLER'S POND (ALSO KNOWN  AS MILLER POND OR POND 1, POND 2, AND POND 3) – STATE GAME LANDS 214

**Location:** Miller's Pond is located in Crawford County, near the town of Linesville and Pymatuning State Park.

**Owner/Manager:** Commonwealth of Pennsylvania/ Pennsylvania Game Commission

**GPS Coordinates:** 41° 36' 34" N, 80° 25' 23" W

**Directions, Access, & Parking:** From the PA-285 causeway, which connects Ohio to Pennsylvania (in the middle of Pymatuning Reservoir), continue east on PA-285 for about 3 miles to the intersection of Hartstown Road. Do not turn onto Hartstown Road but continue straight for less than 1 mile. There will be a dirt road on your left called Swamp Road. Turn down this road until you see the first pond on the right. Continue on this road, and on your right will be a second smaller pond that is near the Food and Cover Building. Park off to the side of the road to view these ponds and surrounding fields. Do not walk or park on the grass on either side of Swamp Road. Swamp Road is not maintained in winter. This road can be very muddy and rutted in early spring and late fall. There is access for cars and buses.

**Site Description:** The Miller's Pond tract, a part of State Game Lands 214, contains deciduous and mixed forests, grassy and farmed fields, and pond areas. The ponds are also known as Pond 1, Pond 2, and Pond 3, although only Pond 1 and Pond 2 are easily viewed from Swamp Road. This area is part of Important Bird Area #3.

**Site Information:** Free admission. This is a controlled hunting area, but wildlife viewing is permitted from the road. Gasoline, restaurants, camping, and convenience/grocery stores are located nearby.

**Key Birds and Wildlife:** Short-billed Dowitcher, Snow Goose, Tundra Swan, Dunlin, Sandhill Crane, Gadwall, Northern Pintail, American Wigeon, Northern Shoveler, Hooded Merganser, Pied-billed Grebe, Ruddy Duck, Greater Yellowlegs, Lesser Yellowlegs, Bald Eagle, Rough-legged Hawk, Horned Lark, Eastern Bluebird, American Kestrel, Eastern Phoebe, Ring-billed Gull, Red-tailed Hawk, Northern Harrier, Eastern Meadowlark, Bobolink, Tree Swallow, Killdeer. When conditions allow for mudflats, sandpipers, plovers, and waders are attracted to the larger pond. Great Egret, Cattle Egret, and American Avocet have even been found here occasionally.

**Other Comments:** The origin of the name for Miller's Pond is unknown. Birders have called it Miller's Pond for years, and the name has stuck. The parking lot of the Pennsylvania Game Commission office farther south along Hartstown Road offers more wildlife viewing. Pymatuning State Park, Linesville State Fish Hatchery, and Wildlife Learning Center are just north of Miller's Pond. Visit www.pgc.state.pa.us for more information.

**Contact Information:**
Pennsylvania Game Commission, Northwest Region
P.O. Box 31
Franklin, PA 16323
(814) 432-3187

Greater Yellowlegs

# 4 STATE GAME LANDS 277

**Location:** State Game Lands 277 is located in Crawford County, near the town of Cambridge Springs.

**Owner/Manager:** Commonwealth of Pennsylvania/ Pennsylvania Game Commission

**GPS Coordinates:** 41° 48' 27" N, 80° 1' 44" W

**Directions, Access, & Parking:** From Cambridge Springs travel north on US-19/US-6, and turn right (east) onto Millers Station Road/SR1016. There is easily accessible parking on site.

**Site Description:** This area of less than 1,000 acres contains mixed mature forest, cultivated fields, many ponds, swamp areas, and a stream. French Creek forms the southern boundary. State Game Lands 277 is part of Important Bird Area #4.

**Site Information:** Free admission. State Game Lands 277 has a well-planned trail system affording close access to the many ponds. Hunting is allowed. Lodging, restaurants, gas stations, and convenience/grocery stores are all nearby.

**Key Birds and Wildlife:** Green-winged Teal, Northern Shoveler, Great Blue Heron, Green Heron, Field Sparrow, Swamp Sparrow, Yellow Warbler, Yellow-breasted Chat, Blue-winged Warbler. This is a good spot to view spring waterfowl during migration.

**Other Comments:** Prior to becoming a game lands, this area was the site of a fish hatchery. Visit www.pgc.state.pa.us for more information.

**Contact Information:**
Pennsylvania Game Commission, Northwest Region
P.O. Box 31
Franklin, PA 16323
(814) 432-3187

## 5 STATE GAME LANDS 435 AND WOODCOCK CREEK LAKE

**Location:** State Game Lands 435 is located in Crawford County, near Saegertown.

**Owner/Manager:** Commonwealth of Pennsylvania/ Pennsylvania Game Commission and United States/United States Army Corps of Engineers

**GPS Coordinates:** 41° 42' 9" N, 80° 6' 2" W
41.702587 N, -80.100715 W

**Directions, Access & Parking:** The park is located at 22079 PA-198. From Meadville drive north about 4.5 miles on N. Main Street/Highway 86. Turn right on PA-198 east; just beyond the dam there are several parking areas. Other access points are farther along PA-198 and south of the lake off of Dickson Road. There is parking for cars and buses. The venue is handicapped accessible.

**Site Description:** Early successional forest, wetlands, and a lake are on the property. The U.S. Army Corps of Engineers manages 1,734 acres (a full reservoir covers 775 acres) on the western end of this site, and the Pennsylvania Game Commission manages about the same amount of land to the east and northeast.

**Site Information:** Free admission. Trailheads are located near the north end of the dam on PA-198 and south of the lake with access from Dickson Road. An observation deck, a visitor center, drinking water, restrooms, picnic shelters, playgrounds, a boat launch ramp, and camping (not in the game lands) are offered around Woodcock Creek Lake. About 1,000 feet of the trail is paved for handicapped accessibility. Hunting is allowed; swimming and motorboating (10 hp limit) are permitted in the lake. Restaurants, lodging, gasoline, campground, and convenience/grocery stores are all nearby.

**Key Birds and Wildlife:** Tundra Swan, Hooded Merganser, Double-crested Cormorant, Osprey, Bald Eagle, Ring-necked Duck, Ruddy Duck, Lesser Scaup, Long-tailed Duck, Field Sparrow, Blue-winged Warbler. State Game Lands 435 is at its best in the spring and fall, when migrating species are in the area. When the lake's water level is lower in late summer and fall, there is excellent habitat for shorebirds. Brant and Piping Plover have been found here.

**Other Comments:** Since the completion of the dam and lake in 1973, Woodcock Creek Lake has provided flood control, improved water quality, and an array of recreational activities. Visit www.pgc.state.pa.us or www.lrp.usace.army.mil/rec/lakes/woodcock.htm for more information.

**Contact Information:**
Woodcock Creek Lake
22079 State Highway 198
Saegertown, PA 16433-0629
(814) 763-4422

Pennsylvania Game Commission, Northwest Region
P.O. Box 31
Franklin, PA 16323
(814) 432-3187

Brant

# 6 STATE GAME LANDS 213:    CUSTARDS

**Location:** State Game Lands 213 is located in Crawford County. The eastern end is near the town of Custards.

**Owner/Manager:** Commonwealth of Pennsylvania/ Pennsylvania Game Commission

**GPS Coordinates:** 41° 32' 17" N, 80° 9' 27" W 41.538061 N, -80.157631 W

**Directions, Access, & Parking:** Take I-79 to Exit 35 (Geneva/Cochranton). Turn right on PA-285 east. Travel for 1.5 miles to the tiny village of Custards. There is a sign on the left side of the road marking the village. Take the first left turn onto a paved road called Mercer Pike. Proceed 0.5 miles until you come to an iron bridge. There is parking on the right side of the road above and below the bridge. There is access for cars and vans and parking for 5–10 vehicles.

**Site Description:** State Game Lands 213 is a long narrow expanse of wetlands along Conneaut Marsh. At the eastern end of Conneaut Marsh there are deciduous forest, shrub/scrub, and plenty of marsh areas. The bridge near Custards provides a convenient viewing platform; walk and bird at both ends and along both sides of the bridge. This area is part of Important Bird Area #7.

**Site Information:** Free admission. Canoeing/ kayaking and hunting are permitted. Gasoline, restaurants, and convenience/grocery stores are located nearby.

**Key Birds and Wildlife:** Bald Eagle, Tundra Swan, Rusty Blackbird, Willow Flycatcher, Eastern Kingbird, Swamp Sparrow, Marsh Wren, Prothonotary Warbler, Sora, Virginia Rail, Least Bittern, Belted Kingfisher, Tree Swallow, Ring-billed Gull, Great Blue Heron, Green Heron, Wilson's Snipe, American Coot, Red-winged Blackbird, Scarlet Tanager, Rose-breasted Grosbeak, Blue-headed Vireo, Red-eyed Vireo, Warbling Vireo, Yellow Warbler, Gray Catbird, Common Moorhen, Wood Duck, Common Yellowthroat, Yellow Warbler. Conneaut Marsh provides important resting and feeding sites for migrating waterfowl and shorebirds. A wide variety of wetland species breed here. Birding is best during spring and fall migrations. In winter birding is usually poor because the marsh freezes. There are beaver and muskrat in the marsh.

**Other Comments:** Locals are used to birders along the road, but be very careful to stay out of the way of the passing cars. Visit www.pgc.state.pa.us for more information.

**Contact Information:**
Pennsylvania Game Commission, Northwest Region
P.O. Box 31
Franklin, PA 16323
(814) 432-3187

*Great Blue Heron*

*Prothonotary Warbler*

## 7 WILDLIFE LEARNING CENTER

**Location:** The Wildlife Learning Center is located in Crawford County, near the town of Linesville and surrounded by Pymatuning State Park.

**Owner/Manager:** Commonwealth of Pennsylvania/ Pennsylvania Game Commission

**GPS Coordinates:** 41° 38' 6" N, 80° 26' 12" W
41.635127 N, -80.436847 W

**Directions, Access, & Parking:** The Wildlife Learning Center at 12590 Hartstown Road is 2 miles south of the town of Linesville. Look for a large wooden sign at the driveway. There is easy access for cars and buses, with parking for more than 10 cars. The site is handicapped accessible; a paved, handicapped-accessible path leads from the center to the parking lot.

**Site Description:** The Wildlife Learning Center contains over 300 mounted specimens of native birds and mammals, some in displays resembling their natural surroundings. The nearby acres contain deciduous and coniferous forests, shrub/ scrub, grassland/savanna, and a lake. The vast section of Pymatuning Lake in front of the Wildlife Learning Center is part of a wildlife propagation area and is limited to only wildlife viewing. This tract is part of Important Bird Area #3.

**Site Information:** Free admission. On-site trails, an observation deck, a visitor center, interpretive signs, restrooms, and drinking water are available. Hands-on activities, environmental education and custom programs, lectures, audios and videos, and guided nature walks are all designed to educate the public about the wilderness and conservation in Pennsylvania. Restaurants, camping, gasoline, and convenience/grocery stores are located close by.

**Key Birds and Wildlife:** Red-tailed Hawk, Tundra Swan, Snow Goose, Double-crested Cormorant, Great Blue Heron, Ring-billed Gull, Bonaparte's Gull, Baltimore Oriole, Yellow Warbler, Turkey Vulture, Red-winged Blackbird, Wood Duck, Black Duck, Red-bellied Woodpecker, Pileated Woodpecker, Northern Flicker, Cedar Waxwing, Warbling Vireo, Cliff Swallow, Winter Wren, Dark-eyed Junco, White-throated Sparrow. This site is one of the best places for observing Bald Eagles in all seasons. Diving ducks can be seen here until the water freezes. The parking lot is a good place to begin birding because of the woody areas bordering it. Tree Swallows and Eastern Bluebirds compete for nesting boxes in front of the learning center. A Purple Martin colony is also found here. White-tailed deer, red fox, and muskrat may be seen here.

**Other Comments:** The Wildlife Learning Center has been in operation since it opened in 1938 as the Pymatuning Museum. The learning center reopens each spring. Visitors are welcome on Thursdays, Fridays, Saturdays, and Sundays from 8:30 a.m. to 4 p.m. Pymatuning State Park, State Game Lands 214, and Linesville State Fish Hatchery are only minutes away.

**Contact Information:**
Wildlife Learning Center
12590 Hartstown Road
Linesville, PA 16424
(814) 683-5545

Pennsylvania Game Commission, Northwest Region
P.O. Box 31
Franklin, PA 16323
(814) 432-3187

Waterfowl

# Elk County

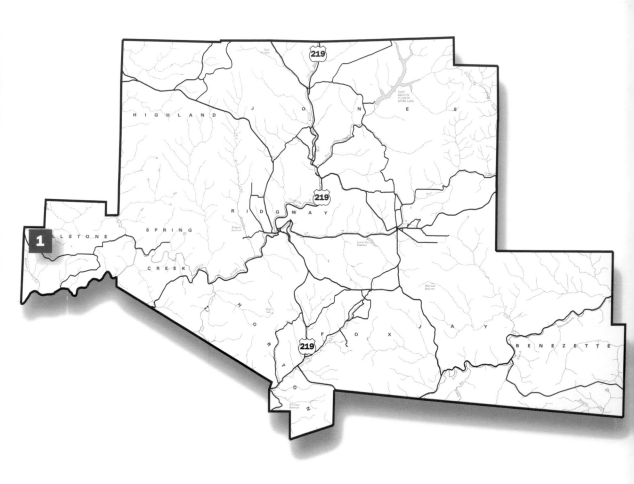

## Legend

 Handicapped Accessibility

 Hiking Trails

 Biking Trails

 Restrooms

 Dogs Allowed

## 1 ALLEGHENY NATIONAL FOREST: BUZZARD SWAMP

**Location:** Buzzard Swamp is located in the Allegheny National Forest, in the counties of Elk and Forest. The nearest town is Marienville.

**Owner/Manager:** United States/United States Department of Agriculture Forest Service

**GPS Coordinates:** 41° 27' 8" N, 79° 5' 22" W

**Directions, Access, & Parking:** From I-80 E toward Clarion, take Exit 60 to merge onto PA-66/Paint Boulevard north toward Shippenville and continue to follow PA-66 for 27.6 miles. Turn right at South Forest Street/SR2005 and continue to follow SR2005 for 1.3 miles. Turn left at Buzzard Swamp Road/Forest Road 157. The southern trailhead to Songbird Sojourn Interpretive Trail and the trail around the swamp and propagation area are located on Forest Road 157. The northern trailhead is located on Forest Road 376, 2.5 miles east of Marienville on Lamonaville Road. Parking for cars is available near trailheads.

**Site Description:** Buzzard Swamp contains a variety of habitats including deciduous, mixed, and early successional forests, shrub/scrub, swamp, lake, pond, and stream areas. Fifteen ponds were built in the 1960s.

**Site Information:** Free admission. The 1.5-mile Songbird Sojourn Interpretive Trail is a self-guided nature trail. About 10 miles of interconnecting trails loop around the many ponds. Information, restrooms, interpretive signage, and camping are available. Mountain biking, canoeing/kayaking, and hunting are permitted. No motorized vehicles or horseback riding are permitted on the trails or in the ponds in Buzzard Swamp. Lodging, restaurants, camping, gas stations, and convenience/grocery stores are all nearby.

**Key Birds and Wildlife:** Brown Creeper, White-breasted Nuthatch, Red-breasted Nuthatch, Golden-crowned Kinglet, Black-capped Chickadee, Common Raven, Dark-eyed Junco, Ruffed Grouse, Alder Flycatcher, American Woodcock, Bobolink, Bald Eagle, Osprey, Red-winged Blackbird, Belted Kingfisher, Ovenbird, Magnolia Warbler, Black-throated Green Warbler, Chestnut-sided Warbler, Hooded Warbler, Common Yellowthroat, Black-and-white Warbler, Field Sparrow, Eastern Meadowlark, Eastern Towhee, Song Sparrow, Rose-breasted Grosbeak, Yellow-bellied Sapsucker, Broad-winged Hawk, Red-tailed Hawk, Green Heron, Hermit Thrush, Scarlet Tanager, Indigo Bunting, Wild Turkey, American Tree Sparrow, Northern Harrier. You might see White-tailed deer, black bear, American beaver, and coyote.

**Other Comments:** Mosquitoes can be very bad during summer months. Some trails have little protection from sun and wind. Visit www.fs.fed.us/r9/forests/allegheny for more information.

**Contact Information:**
Allegheny National Forest
4 Farm Colony Drive
Warren, PA 16365
(814) 723-5150

Bradford Ranger District
Star Route, Box 88
Bradford, PA 16701
(814) 362-4613

*Belted Kingfisher*

# Erie County

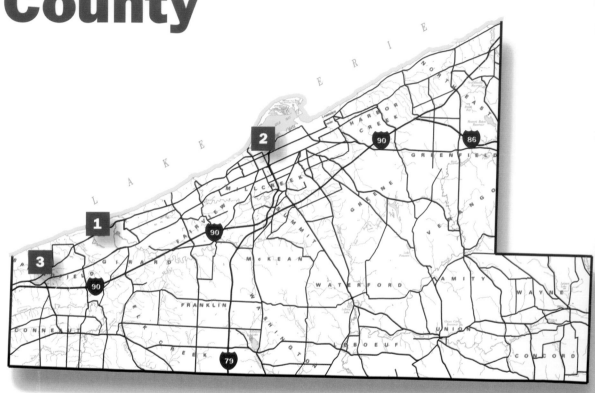

## Legend

 Handicapped Accessibility

 Hiking Trails

 Biking Trails

 Restrooms

 Dogs Allowed

## 1 ERIE BLUFFS STATE PARK

**Location:** Erie Bluffs State Park is located in Erie County, near the borough of Lake City.

**Owner/Manager:** Commonwealth of Pennsylvania/ Pennsylvania Department of Conservation and Natural Resources

**GPS Coordinates:** 42° 1' 11" N, 80° 22' 27" W

**Directions, Access, & Parking:** From Erie, drive west on PA-5 to Lake City. Look for the Elk Creek Fishing area on the right, leading to the Elk Creek Marina and parking lot. From the lot there is a trail which leads west to Erie Bluffs State Park. Limited parking is available for cars and buses.

**Site Description:** The 540-acre Erie Bluffs State Park contains deciduous and early successional forests, wetlands of exceptional value, cultivated fields, barrens, lake, and stream areas. The park is home to one mile of undeveloped Lake Erie shoreline. The 90-foot-high bluffs provide views of the lake, and the area contains an uncommon oak savanna sand barren ecosystem. Some rare, endangered, and threatened flora grow here.

**Site Information:** Free admission. On-site trails. There are currently no facilities in the park. Lodging, restaurants, campgrounds, gasoline, and convenience stores are close by.

**Key Birds and Wildlife:** Bald Eagle, Caspian Tern, Osprey, Bank Swallow, Purple Martin, Great Blue Heron, Killdeer, Red-headed Woodpecker, Acadian Flycatcher, Eastern Kingbird, Warbling Vireo, Veery, Cedar Waxwing, Mourning Warbler, American Redstart, Scarlet Tanager, Vesper Sparrow, Indigo Bunting. The adjacent Elk Run Creek is known for world class steelhead trout fishing.

**Other Comments:** Erie Bluffs State Park is the newest Pennsylvania State Park. It contains significant archaeological sites. Visit www.dcnr.state.pa.us/stateparks for more information.

**Contact Information:**
Erie Bluffs State Park
c/o Presque Isle State Park
Erie, PA 16505
(814) 833-7424

Black Tern

# 2 PRESQUE ISLE STATE PARK AND TOM RIDGE ENVIRONMENTAL CENTER

**Location:** Presque Isle State Park is located in Erie County, near the City of Erie.

**Owner/Manager:** Commonwealth of Pennsylvania/ Pennsylvania Department of Conservation and Natural Resources

**GPS Coordinates:** 42° 6' 27" N, 80° 9' 12" W

**Directions, Access, & Parking:** The Tom Ridge Environmental Center and Presque Isle State Park can be reached by PA-832 off of I-79 N. Travel I-79 N towards Erie and take Exit 183B to merge onto W 12th Street/PA-5 W toward US-20. Turn right at PA-832 N/Peninsula Drive. The entrance to the environmental center will be on your right. Continue straight to enter the park. There is access for cars and buses, and ample parking exists throughout the park. The park may also be reached by boat.

**Site Description:** The 3,000-acre Presque Isle State Park contains deciduous, coniferous, and early successional forests, shrub/scrub, swamp, intertidal wetlands, riparian, lake, pond, and beach areas. Presque Isle State Park has been designated as Important Bird Area #1. This site is truly one of the best in the region—over 330 species have been tallied at this location.

**Site Information:** Free admission. The road system within the park forms a loop approximately 13 miles in length. On-site trails, observation decks, a visitor center, restrooms, environmental education programs, custom programs, and drinking water are available. Tom Ridge Environmental Center is open seven days a week, year round from 10 a.m. to 6 p.m. Mountain biking, motor boating, canoeing/kayaking, jet skiing, organized sports, and hunting are permitted. Gasoline, lodging, restaurants, camping, and convenience/grocery stores are located nearby.

**Key Birds and Wildlife:** Long-eared Owl, Northern Saw-whet Owl, Osprey, Bald Eagle, Red-throated Loon, White-winged Scoter, Black Scoter, Surf Scoter, Sora, Virginia Rail, Least Bittern, American Bittern, Bonaparte's Gull, Little Gull, Great Black-backed Gull, Caspian Tern, Black Tern, Ruddy Turnstone, Sanderling, Red-headed Woodpecker, Swainson's Thrush, Gray-cheeked Thrush, Alder Flycatcher, Yellow-bellied Flycatcher, Blackpoll Warbler, Baltimore Oriole, Purple Martin, Warbling Vireo, Philadelphia Vireo, Northern Waterthrush, Wilson's Warbler, Lincoln's Sparrow, White-crowned Sparrow, Snow Bunting, Common Redpoll.

**Other Comments:** Presque Isle is arguably the state's premier birding site and is one of the top 10 national sites, according to *Birder's World* magazine. The area attracts exceptional numbers of migrants but also an unusual array of vagrant birds. Recommended trails include: Pine Tree Trail, Fry's Landing, Thompson Circle, Sidewalk Trail, Dead Pond Trail, Long Pond Trail. Beach 11 and Thompson Bay are often excellent for waterfowl and gulls during migration. Visit www.dcnr.state.pa.us/stateparks for more information.

**Contact Information:**
Tom Ridge Environmental Center (Park Office)
301 Peninsula Drive, Suite 1
Erie, PA 16505
(814) 833-7424

Little Gull

## 3 STATE GAME LANDS 314
## RODERICK TRACT (ALSO KNOWN
## AS DAVID M. RODERICK WILDLIFE RESERVE)

**Location:** State Game Lands 314 is located in Erie County, near the town of Conneaut, Ohio.

**Owner/Manager:** Commonwealth of Pennsylvania/ Pennsylvania Game Commission

**GPS Coordinates:** 41° 57' 22" N, 80° 29' 36" W

**Directions, Access, & Parking:** From the City of Erie, drive west on I-90 to the US-6 N exit. Drive north on US-6 N to US-20, then turn left (west) on US-20 and proceed to the point where US-20 merges with PA-5. Immediately turn right on Rudd Road, which leads into the middle of the game lands. Parking is available for cars and vans.

**Site Description:** The 3,131-acre State Game Lands 314 contains mixed and early successional forests, shrub/ scrub, marsh, lake, pond, stream, and bluff areas. The tract has the longest undeveloped stretch of scenic bluffs along Lake Erie's south shore. Several roads crisscross the land to provide access to wildlife viewing points. The area has been designated as Important Bird Area #2.

**Site Information:** Free admission. Hikers may need rubber boots on the trails in the wet season. Hunting is permitted. Lodging, restaurants, camping, gasoline, and convenience stores are nearby.

**Key Birds and Wildlife:** Bald Eagle, Osprey, Caspian Tern, Northern Bobwhite, Bank Swallow, Cliff Swallow, American Woodcock, Red-shouldered Hawk, Cooper's Hawk, Ruby-throated Hummingbird, Northern Flicker, Eastern Phoebe, Eastern Kingbird, Veery, Cedar Waxwing, Chipping Sparrow, Red-winged Blackbird, Indigo Bunting. In the bluffs overlooking Lake Erie, there is a large colony of Bank Swallows. The overlook near the David M. Roderick Monument is a good place to watch migrating gulls, terns, and raptors. Check flocks of Cedar Waxwings in winter for the occasional Bohemian Waxwing. It is possible to tally 100 species here on a good day in April.

**Other Comments:** David M. Roderick, for whom the reserve is named, was the CEO of United States Steel from 1979 to 1989. He was an avid outdoorsman who started the process by which the land belonging to U.S. Steel was eventually transferred to the Pennsylvania Game Commission. The David M. Roderick Wildlife Reserve was dedicated in 1991. Visit www.pgc.state.pa.us for more information.

**Contact Information:**
Pennsylvania Game Commission, Northwest Region
P.O. Box 31
Franklin, PA 16323
(814) 432-3187

Red-tailed Hawk

# Fayette County

## Legend

 Handicapped Accessibility

 Hiking Trails

 Biking Trails

 Restrooms

 Dogs Allowed

## 1 BEAR RUN NATURE RESERVE

**Location:** Bear Run Nature Reserve is in Fayette County, near the town of Mill Run and just northeast of Ohiopyle.

**Owner/Manager:** Western Pennsylvania Conservancy

**GPS Coordinates:** 39° 54' 23" N, 79° 27' 37" W

**Directions, Access, & Parking:** From I-76/PA Turnpike, take Exit 91 (Donegal). Turn left onto PA-31 east, then right onto PA-711 south (Jones Mill Road). Follow PA-711 for 9.6 miles. Turn left onto Mill Run Road/PA-381. Continue for 6.1 miles to a large barn and parking lot on the left. Parking is available for cars and buses.

**Site Description:** The 5,200-acre Bear Run Nature Reserve is home to deciduous, coniferous, mixed, and early successional forests, shrub/scrub, grassland/savanna, fallow fields, riparian, river, and stream areas. The extensive trail system at Bear Run Nature Reserve allows visitors to access a variety of bird habitats. Two high-gradient streams, Laurel Run and Bear Run, provide habitat for a wide variety of interior forest bird species. Additionally, agricultural fields planted with warm and cool season grasses provide habitat for grassland nesting birds. Bear Run Nature Reserve has been designated as Important Bird Area #26.

**Site Information:** Free admission. On-site trails and camping are available. Horseback riding and hunting are permitted. Lodging, campgrounds, restaurants, and convenience stores are nearby. Pets and motorized vehicles are not permitted on the reserve.

**Key Birds and Wildlife:** Ovenbird, Hooded Warbler, Scarlet Tanager, Black-throated Green Warbler, Black-throated Blue Warbler, Blackburnian Warbler, Black-and-white Warbler, Canada Warbler, Louisiana Waterthrush, Ruffed Grouse, Acadian Flycatcher, Wood Thrush.

**Other Comments:** The original reserve of 500 acres and Edgar Kaufmann's family house, Fallingwater, were entrusted to the Western Pennsylvania Conservancy in 1963. The WPC has since acquired over 5,000 acres. Fallingwater is Frank Lloyd Wright's renowned monument to organic architecture; plan a tour if time permits. Visit www.fallingwater.org for more information.

**Contact Information:**
Fallingwater
1478 Mill Run Road
Mill Run PA 15464
(724) 329-7803

Indigo Bunting

# 2 OHIOPYLE STATE PARK

**Location:** Ohiopyle State Park is in Fayette County, near the town of Ohiopyle.

**Owner/Manager:** Commonwealth of Pennsylvania/ Pennsylvania Department of Conservation and Natural Resources

**GPS Coordinates:** 39° 52' 13" N, 79° 29' 35" W

**Directions, Access, & Parking:** From Exit 91 of I-76/Pennsylvania Turnpike, follow PA-31 east for two miles, then turn right onto PA-711/PA-381 south. Travel for 10 miles through the town of Normalville, then turn left to continue on PA-381 south for 10 more miles until you reach Ohiopyle State Park. Parking is available for cars and buses. The venue is handicapped accessible.

**Site Description:** Ohiopyle State Park encompasses 19,052 acres. Deciduous, coniferous with many hemlocks, and mixed forests, shrub/scrub, grassland/savanna, rocky bank, steep hillside, wetland, stream, river, rapids, and five waterfall areas offer a variety of habitats for species that favor higher elevations. Ohiopyle State Park is part of Important Bird Area #26.

**Site Information:** Free admission. Seventy-nine miles of trails, restrooms, drinking water, interpretive signage, a gift shop and snack bar, overlook platforms, camping, and environmental education programs are offered. Horseback riding, biking (with an overnight car park), mountain biking, canoeing/kayaking, whitewater boating (class I through class IV), picnicking, rock climbing, snowmobiling, cross-country skiing, and sledding occur on site. Hunting and trapping are allowed here and at adjacent game lands. Lodging, restaurants, campgrounds, and convenience/grocery stores are all nearby.

**Key Birds and Wildlife:** Worm-eating Warbler, Kentucky Warbler, Wild Turkey, White-throated Sparrow, American Tree Sparrow, Dark-eyed Junco, Common Merganser, Turkey Vulture, Spotted Sandpiper, Red-eyed Vireo, Yellow-throated Vireo, Blue-headed Vireo, White-eyed Vireo, Pileated Woodpecker, Eastern Phoebe, Cliff Swallow, Barn Swallow, Wood Thrush, Cedar Waxwing, Indigo Bunting, Rose-breasted Grosbeak, Chipping Sparrow, Song Sparrow. Golden-winged Warbler has been located here in the recent past. The forest supports a wide variety of breeding neotropical migrants, while a brushy area near the campground is a good place to locate breeding American Woodcock, Ruffed Grouse, Prairie Warbler, Yellow-breasted Chat, and other species. White-tailed deer, black bear, coyote, and river otter can be seen. A river otter reintroduction program was conducted here. The Youghiogheny River is a good trout stream.

**Other Comments:** The Youghiogheny River Gorge and surrounding mountains offer breathtaking scenery. The 14 miles of river gorge contain some of the most challenging whitewater rapids in the state, but the noise can hamper birders. The Youghiogheny River Trail, part of the Great Allegheny Passage, has 27 miles of trail in the park. Visit www.dcnr.state.pa.us/stateparks for more information.

**Contact Information:**
Ohiopyle State Park
124 Main Street
Ohiopyle, PA 15470
(724) 329-8591

House Wren

*Yellow-rumped Warbler*

# Forest County

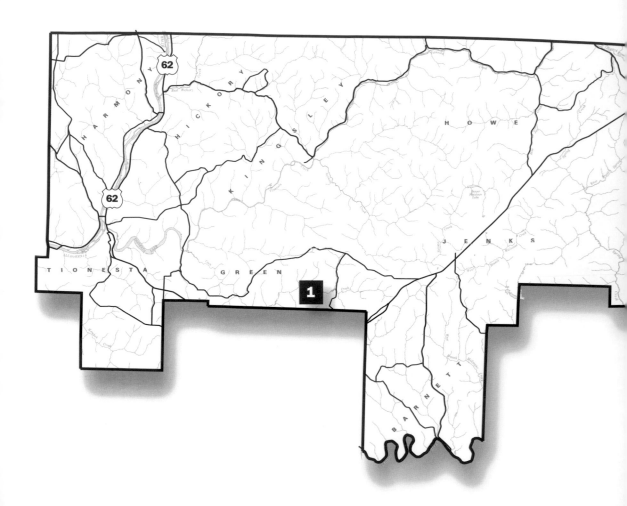

## Legend

 Handicapped Accessibility  Hiking Trails  Biking Trails  Restrooms  Dogs Allowed

## 1 ALLEGHENY NATIONAL FOREST: SALMON CREEK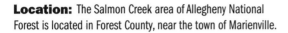

**Location:** The Salmon Creek area of Allegheny National Forest is located in Forest County, near the town of Marienville.

**Owner/Manager:** United States/United States Department of Agriculture Forest Service

**GPS Coordinates:** 41° 27' 32" N, 79° 11' 16" W

**Directions, Access, & Parking:** From Marienville drive southwest on PA-66 for 2 miles to the town of Roses. Bear right on SR3004 (Oak Woods/Gultonville/Muzette Road) and drive west for 1.5 miles. Turn right on Salmon Creek Road (FR145), which descends into the Salmon Creek Valley. Parking is available along the road for cars. Be aware that the road is rough.

**Site Description:** Salmon Creek contains deciduous, coniferous, mixed, and early successional forests and stream areas. This is an uninhabited region of the Allegheny National Forest; part of the North Country Trail runs through the valley. There is a clean trout stream and large, pure stands of hemlock.

**Site Information:** Free admission. On-site trails are available. Camping, fishing, and hunting are permitted at this location. Lodging, restaurants, a campground, and convenience stores can be found in Marienville.

**Key Birds and Wildlife:** Swainson's Thrush, Common Raven, Winter Wren, Yellow-bellied Sapsucker, Barred Owl, Common Merganser, Purple Finch, Great Blue Heron, Yellow-billed Cuckoo, Acadian Flycatcher, Hermit Thrush, Magnolia Warbler, Black-throated Green Warbler, Ovenbird, Dark-eyed Junco, Indigo Bunting.

**Other Comments:** Cell phone reception is limited, and there are no restrooms, water, or other facilities. Visit www.fs.fed.us/r9/forests/allegheny for more information.

**Contact Information:**
Allegheny National Forest
4 Farm Colony Drive
Warren, PA 16365
(814) 723-5150

Rough-legged Hawk

# Fulton County

## Legend

 Handicapped Accessibility

 Hiking Trails

 Biking Trails

 Restrooms

 Dogs Allowed

## 1 HAINES-SEVILLE WETLANDS

**Location:** Haines-Seville Wetlands is located in Fulton County, near the town of McConnellsburg and 1 mile south of Harrisonville.

**Owner/Manager:** Commonwealth of Pennsylvania/ Pennsylvania Department of Transportation

**GPS Coordinates:** 39° 58' 26" N, 78° 4' 6" W

**Directions, Access, & Parking:** From Pittsburgh take the PA Turnpike/I-76 E towards Harrisburg. Take the exit onto I-70 E towards US-30 and Breezewood. Continue on US-30/Lincoln Highway east for 11 miles and turn right (south) onto PA-655/Pleasant Ridge Road. After 1.1 miles, look for the entrance sign and parking lot on the left. Parking is available for cars and buses.

**Site Description:** Haines-Seville Wetlands is a 20-acre transitioning ephemeral wetland built by the Pennsylvania Department of Transportation. PennDOT mows a path around the perimeter.

**Site Information:** Free admission. A picnic pavilion, birdhouses, and bat boxes overlook the wetland. Gasoline, restaurants, lodging, and convenience/grocery stores are located nearby.

**Key Birds and Wildlife:** In the spring watch for migrating ducks, rails, bitterns, Wilson's Snipe, and Rusty Blackbird. Wood Duck, Green Heron, Pied-billed Grebe, and Tree Swallow can be found when sufficient water remains in the summer. Vesper Sparrow, Grasshopper Sparrow, and finches feed in the surrounding fields in the fall. Rare visitors include Snow Goose, Great Egret, Trumpeter Swan, Ring-necked Duck, and Marsh Wren.

**Other Comments:** You might need rubber boots to walk the grassy path around the southern part of the wetlands.

**Contact Information:**
Pennsylvania Dept. of Transportation, Fulton County
22907 Great Cove Road
P.O. Box 656
McConnellsburg, PA 17233
(717) 485-3816

Blue-winged Teal

# Indiana County

## Legend

 Handicapped
Accessibility

 Hiking
Trails

 Biking
Trails

 Restrooms

 Dogs
Allowed

# 1 CONEMAUGH DAM AND CONEMAUGH RIVER LAKE

**Location:** Conemaugh Dam and Conemaugh River Lake are located in Indiana County, seven miles southeast of the town of Saltsburg.

**Owner/Manager:** United States/United States Army Corps of Engineers

**GPS Coordinates:** 40° 28' 0" N, 79° 22' 7" W

**Directions, Access, & Parking:** From Pittsburgh, take I-376 E towards Monroeville. The highway becomes US-22 E. Continue for 18 miles and then turn left onto PA-981 north at New Alexandria. Continue on PA-981 north for 4.7 miles and turn right onto Tunnelton Road. Follow Tunnelton Road; after crossing the bridge over the Conemaugh River, continue for almost 1 mile and turn right onto Auen Road. The entrance to the Conemaugh River Lake will be 0.7 miles on the right. Parking is available for cars and buses.

**Site Description:** The 975-foot-tall and 1,265-foot-wide Conemaugh Dam is a concrete gravity dam. The lake behind the dam ranges from 6,820 acres when it is full to 800 acres during the summer. The Pennsylvania Game Commission leases 7,000 acres around the lake for wildlife management.

**Site Information:** Free admission. Information, observation deck, visitor center, restrooms, drinking water, guided tours through the dam, two pavilions and interpretive signage are available. Biking is popular on the nearby West Penn Trail. Canoeing/kayaking and fishing are permitted on the lake; hunting is permitted in the surrounding area. Adjacent to the dam, the Bow Ridge Recreation Area offers trails excellent for hiking and observing nature by foot or bicycle. Tunnelview Historic Site, directly downstream of the dam, provides a self-guided historic walk along a section of the restored Main Line Canal that once connected Philadelphia to Pittsburgh (1834–1854). Restaurants, gasoline, and convenience stores are nearby.

**Key Birds and Wildlife:** Waterfowl can be abundant during fall migration including Bufflehead, Hooded Merganser, Common Merganser, Redhead, Canvasback, and Northern Pintail. Tree Swallow and Northern Rough-winged Swallow are also common species. Yellow-throated Warbler can be found in the breeding season. There is a watchable wildlife site located behind the dam's visitor center. A newly installed bat-roosting box provides visitors with the opportunity to note the new box design and proper selection of an installation site. Environmental education programs are provided in the summer months.

**Other Comments:** Conemaugh Dam was completed in 1952 and has since prevented over $2 billion in damage from floods. Hurricane Ivan struck the area in 2004, and this dam alone prevented $375 million in damage. Flood levels in Pittsburgh can be reduced by four feet by the dam. For daily lake and recreation information, call (724) 639-3785. Visit www.lrp.usace.army.mil/rec/lakes/conemaugh.htm for more information.

**Contact Information:**
Conemaugh River Lake
1665 Auen Road, Suite A
RD 2, Box 131
Saltsburg, PA 15681
(724) 459-7240

Willet

# 2 WEST PENN TRAIL

**Location:** The West Penn Trail is a 17-mile rail-trail between Saltsburg and Blairsville in Indiana and Westmoreland counties.

**Owner/Manager:** Conemaugh Valley Conservancy

**GPS Coordinates:** 40° 28' 54" N, 79° 26' 51" W

**Directions, Access, & Parking:** From Pittsburgh take I-376 E towards Monroeville; the highway becomes US-22 E. Continue for 18 miles to PA-981 N at New Alexandria. Turn left onto PA-981 N and continue for 8 miles. Make a right onto PA-286, cross the bridge, and turn right onto Salt Street. Continue until you reach the trailhead and parking. Parking is available for cars and buses.

**Site Description:** The West Penn Trail is an important tie in a 320-mile corridor linking history and outdoor recreation from Pittsburgh to Harrisburg. The Conemaugh River, alongside the trail, has seen an increase in avian and other species, including 53 species of wildflowers. The area contains deciduous forest, riparian, lake, pond, river, and stream areas.

**Site Information:** Free admission. Self-guided trails, an observation deck, restrooms, drinking water, interpretive signage, and a community park are available. Horseback riding, biking, canoeing/kayaking, hunting, fishing, and leashed pets are allowed. Upstream from the Conemaugh Dam, the trail may not be accessible due to high water, especially in the spring. Lodging, restaurants, campgrounds, and convenience/grocery stores are all nearby.

**Key Birds and Wildlife:** Wood Duck, Northern Harrier, Red-tailed Hawk, American Kestrel, Red-bellied Woodpecker, Northern Flicker, Pileated Woodpecker, Black-capped Chickadee, Carolina Chickadee, Tufted Titmouse, Carolina Wren, Northern Mockingbird, Dark-eyed Junco, Brown-headed Cowbird, Pine Siskin. Mammals along the trail include bats, muskrat, American beaver, and American mink.

**Other Comments:** The West Penn Trail generally follows a scenic and historic route used by the Pennsylvania Main Line Canal and Portage Railroad. Points of historical interest are marked by interpretive signs. Visit www.conemaughvalleyconservancy.org for more information.

**Contact Information:**
Conemaugh Valley Conservancy
P.O. Box 502
Hollsopple, PA 15935

## 3  YELLOW CREEK STATE PARK

**Location:** Yellow Creek State Park is located in Indiana County, near the town of Penn Run.

**Owner/Manager:** Commonwealth of Pennsylvania/Pennsylvania Department of Conservation and Natural Resources

**GPS Coordinates:** 40° 34' 41" N, 79° 0' 2" W

**Directions, Access, & Parking:** From Indiana, Pa., take US-422 east toward Ebensburg. Turn right onto PA-259 and proceed 0.15 miles to the park office on the right. Parking is available.

**Site Description:** Yellow Creek State Park covers 3,140 acres and contains deciduous, coniferous, and early successional forests, shrub/scrub, marsh, riparian, lake, pond, and stream areas. Yellow Creek State Park has been designated as Important Bird Area #23.

**Site Information:** Free admission. On-site trails, an observation blind, a visitor center, restrooms, drinking water, and interpretive signage are available. Educational programs are offered to the public from April 1 to October 31. Canoeing/ kayaking provides a fantastic way to view this site. Camping and hunting are permitted.

**Key Birds and Wildlife:** Northern Harrier, Brown Creeper, Golden-crowned Kinglet, Swamp Sparrow, Tundra Swan, Osprey, Bald Eagle, Red-throated Loon, Common Loon, Caspian Tern, Forster's Tern, Green Heron, Willow Flycatcher, Blue-headed Vireo, Blackburnian Warbler, Louisiana Waterthrush, Purple Finch, Wilson's Snipe, Fox Sparrow, Lincoln's Sparrow. Yellow Creek State Park's close proximity to Chestnut Ridge allows for viewing of large numbers of waterfowl and gulls stopping to usc thc lake.

**Other Comments:** It is recommended that birders stay off the trails during hunting season. Visit www.dcnr.state.pa.us/stateparks for more information.

### Contact Information:
Yellow Creek State Park
170 Route 259 Highway
Penn Run, PA 15765
(724) 357-7913

*Bonaparte's Gull*

*Red-necked Grebe*

# Jefferson County

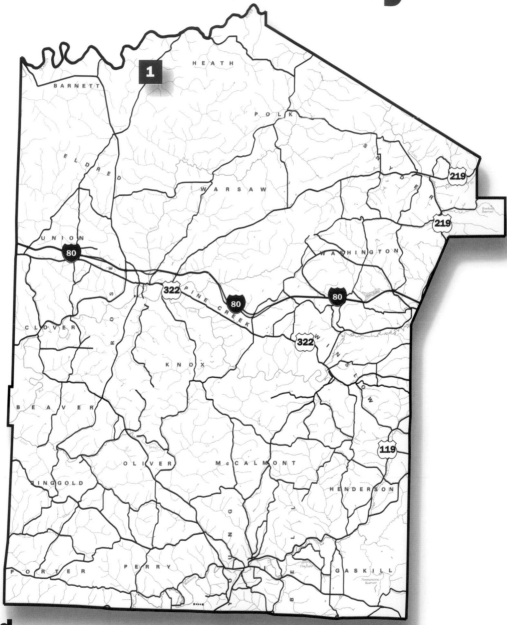

## Legend

 Handicapped Accessibility

 Hiking Trails

 Biking Trails

 Restrooms

 Dogs Allowed

## 1 CLEAR CREEK STATE PARK AND STATE FOREST

**Location:** Clear Creek State Park and Clear Creek State Forest are located in Jefferson County, northeast of Clarion and near the town of Sigel.

**Owner/Manager:** Commonwealth of Pennsylvania/Pennsylvania Department of Conservation and Natural Resources

**GPS Coordinates:** 41° 19' 25" N, 79° 4' 43" W

**Directions, Access, & Parking:** From I-80 E near Corsica, take Exit 73 for PA-949 north. Follow PA-949 for about 12 miles to the park entrance. Make a left turn into the state park or a right turn into the state forest. Or from I-80 W near Brookville, take Exit 78. Turn right at PA-36/Allegheny Boulevard and proceed north for 7.4 miles. Turn right at PA-949/Clear Creek Road and continue north for about 4 miles. Make a left turn into the state park or a right turn into the state forest. Small parking lots are strategically scattered along the park and forest roads to provide access to facilities, scenery, and trailheads. There is ample parking for cars and buses. Some facilities and campsites are designated as handicapped accessible.

**Site Description:** Clear Creek State Park and Clear Creek State Forest are home to deciduous, coniferous, and mixed forests, river, lake, and stream areas. The area contains large stands of hemlock trees and has a number of breeding birds more typical of northern forests. The state park contains 1,676 acres and the adjacent state forest has 9,089 acres. There are other smaller parcels also designated as Clear Creek State Forest in Venango and Forest counties.

**Site Information:** Free admission. Twenty-five miles of well-maintained trails loop through the park and continue into the forest. Information, restrooms, drinking water, and interpretive signs are available. Environmental educators provide guided walks in the summer and evening campfire programs. Swimming in a man-made lake, mountain biking, cross-country skiing, hunting, trapping, fishing, canoeing/kayaking, and picnicking are permitted. There are campsites in the state park.

**Key Birds and Wildlife:** Ruffed Grouse, Green Heron, Cooper's Hawk, Wild Turkey, Killdeer, Ruby-throated Hummingbird, Hairy Woodpecker, Eastern Wood-Pewee, White-breasted Nuthatch, Northern Parula, Chestnut-sided Warbler, American Redstart, Blackburnian Warbler, Canada Warbler, Indigo Bunting, Common Grackle, Northern Rough-winged Swallow, Golden-crowned Kinglet, Yellow-bellied Sapsucker, Blue-headed Vireo, Common Raven, Winter Wren, Hermit Thrush, Dark-eyed Junco. Clear Creek has both native and stocked brook trout. White-tailed deer and black bear may be seen in the area.

**Other Comments:** Clear Creek State Park was opened in 1922, and many of the facilities and attractions were expanded by the Civilian Conservation Corps between 1933 and 1937. The park occupies a scenic portion of the Clear Creek Valley from the Clarion River to PA-949; it is especially beautiful when the deciduous trees turn colors in the fall. The blooming rhododendron and mountain laurel are spectacular in the spring. Visit www.dcnr.state.pa.us/stateparks for more information.

**Contact Information:**
Clear Creek State Park
38 Clear Creek Park Road
Sigel, PA 15860
(814) 752-2368

PA Bureau of Forestry, Forest District #8
158 South Second Avenue
Clarion, PA 16214-1904
(814) 226-1901

*Common Grackle*

# Lawrence County

## Legend

 Handicapped Accessibility

 Hiking Trails

 Biking Trails

 Restrooms

 Dogs Allowed

# 1 McCONNELLS MILL STATE PARK

**Location:** McConnells Mill State Park is located in Lawrence County, near the town of Portersville and about 40 miles north of Pittsburgh.

**Owner/Manager:** Commonwealth of Pennsylvania/ Pennsylvania Department of Conservation and Natural Resources

**GPS Coordinates:** 40° 57' 4" N, 80° 10' 4" W

**Directions, Access, & Parking:** From Pittsburgh, take I-79 N to Exit 96. Turn left on PA-488 and drive 0.6 miles to PA-19. Turn right on PA-19 and travel 1.5 miles to Killdoo Road. Turn left and continue 1.2 miles to the main parking lot. Parking is available for cars and buses.

**Site Description:** The 2,546-acre McConnells Mill State Park is home to mixed and early successional forests, shrub/scrub, riparian, and stream areas. The site centers on Slippery Rock Creek Gorge with its excellent white-water stream. The steep, wooded, rocky hillsides have many hemlocks. McConnells Mill State Park has been designated as Important Birding Area #77.

**Site Information:** Free admission. Information, restrooms, drinking water, and interpretive signage are available. The park has 11 miles of trails, including part of the North Country Trail. Canoeing/kayaking, rafting, rappelling in two designated climbing areas, hunting, fishing, and trapping are permitted. Lodging, restaurants, camping, gasoline, and convenience stores are nearby.

**Key Birds and Wildlife:** Ruffed Grouse, Wild Turkey, Winter Wren, Blue-headed Vireo, Black-throated Green Warbler, Louisiana Waterthrush, Wood Duck, Northern Harrier, Killdeer, Spotted Sandpiper, Willow Flycatcher, Red-eyed Vireo, White-breasted Nuthatch, American Redstart, Common Yellowthroat, Chipping Sparrow, Savannah Sparrow, Purple Finch, Baltimore Oriole. The cool, damp habitat supports many birds usually found in Canada.

**Other Comments:** The gristmill that operated in the 1800s and closed in 1928 is open for in-season tours. The park is open year-round from sunrise to sunset. Exercise extreme caution on steep terrain, slippery rocks, and beware of swift currents. Visit www.dcnr.state.pa.us/stateparks for more information.

**Contact Information:**
McConnells Mill State Park
c/o Moraine State Park
225 Pleasant Valley Road
Portersville, PA 16051
(724) 368-8811

Savannah Sparrow

# 2 THE VOLANT STRIPS

**Location:** The Volant Strips are located in Lawrence County, near the town of Volant.

**Owner/Manager:** Private property

**GPS Coordinates:** 41° 6' 17" N, 80° 11' 54" W

**Directions, Access, & Parking:** Take I-79 N to the Grove City/PA-208 exit. Turn left onto PA-208 and pass the outlet mall. Turn left onto Veteran's Road/TR315 and follow to its end at Brent Road. Turn left onto Brent Road and make the first right onto Number 2 Mine Road. Follow Number 2 Mine Road, crossing over Pennsy Swamp, to its end at Nelson Road. Turn left onto Nelson Road. The Volant Strips begin on either side of Nelson Road; scan the fields that continue for about 1 mile. Birders may opt to explore nearby county and township roads. Black Swamp is located 0.5 miles east of Nelson Road. From Nelson turn east onto Black Road and go to a small parking entrance on the left. The swamp is located a few hundred feet beyond the parking area. To search for Sandhill Cranes continue east on Black Road and north on Old Ash Road. Stop at the intersection with Bonanni Road and check the surrounding fields.

**Site Description:** The 1,000-acre Volant Strips contain deciduous forest, grassland/savanna, cultivated and fallow fields, swamp, and pond areas. The Volant Strips are part of Important Bird Area #10.

**Site Information:** This is private property; birding takes place from the road. Hunting occurs in the area in late fall and winter. Gasoline, camping, and restaurants are located nearby.

**Key Birds and Wildlife:** Snow Bunting, Horned Lark, Henslow's Sparrow, Grasshopper Sparrow, Bobolink, Eastern Meadowlark, Short-eared Owl, American Kestrel, Northern Harrier. Waterfowl and woodland species such as Black-throated Green Warbler, Hooded Warbler, and Red-eyed Vireo can be found here. A resident flock of Sandhill Cranes is often found. Spring and fall are the easiest times to see the cranes, but large flocks are often seen in the winter.

**Other Comments:** Please respect private property and remain on the roads. The Volant Strips are so named because they were formerly strip mines in the Volant area.

**Contact Information:** Private property

*American Kestrel*

# Mercer County

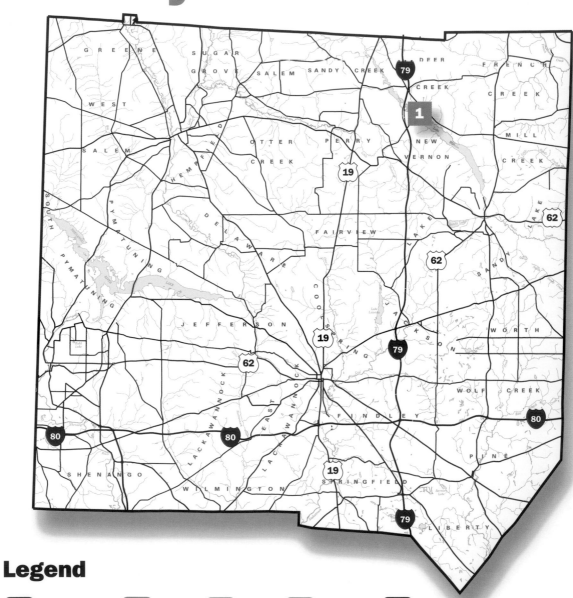

## Legend

 Handicapped Accessibility

 Hiking Trails

Biking Trails

 Restrooms

 Dogs Allowed

# 1 STATE GAME LANDS 270 AND MAURICE K. GODDARD STATE PARK

**Location:** State Game Lands 270 is located in Mercer County, near the town of Sandy Lake.

**Owner/Manager:** Commonwealth of Pennsylvania/ Pennsylvania Department of Conservation and Natural Resources and Pennsylvania Game Commission

**GPS Coordinates:** 41° 25′ 11″ N, 80° 9′ 21″ W

**Directions, Access, & Parking:** From I-79, take Exit 130 (Sandy Lake/Greenville) and travel west on PA-358 (towards Greenville) for about 0.1 miles, then bear right onto Sheakleyville Road. At the first stop sign, turn right onto Lake Wilhelm Road, which goes directly to the park. Parking is available for cars and buses, and the venue is handicapped accessible.

**Site Description:** Maurice K. Goddard State Park consists of 2,856 acres, including 1,860-acre Lake Wilhelm. State Game Lands 270 is 2,027 acres; it covers the area surrounding the lake and west of I-79. Mixed mature forest, cultivated fields, swamp, marsh, and stream areas make up the remainder of the game lands and park not covered by Lake Wilhelm. Maurice K. Goddard State Park has been designated as Important Bird Area #79.

**Site Information:** Free admission. Fourteen miles of hiking trails, an observation deck, an observation blind, a visitor center, picnic pavilions, restrooms, drinking water, interpretive signs, camping, and environmental programs are offered in the park. Hunting is allowed. Bicycling is permitted on the South Shore Trail. Boating (electric motors only in the game lands) and canoeing/kayaking are allowed on the lake. Restaurants, campground, and convenience/grocery stores are all nearby.

**Key Birds and Wildlife:** American Woodcock, Wilson's Snipe, Pileated Woodpecker, Eastern Bluebird, Purple Martin, Common Nighthawk, Common Loon, Common Goldeneye, Bufflehead, Blue-winged Teal, Green-winged Teal, Hooded Merganser, Common Merganser. State Game Lands 270 is an excellent spot to view waterfowl. Osprey and Bald Eagles actively nest in the area.

**Other Comments:** McKeever Environmental Learning Center is located at the eastern end of the park and offers residential and non-residential programs throughout the year. The 205 acres and 4 miles of trails offer a peaceful getaway; they are open to the public from sunrise to sunset. The center is administered as a public service by Slippery Rock University. Visit www.dcnr.state.pa.us/stateparks or www.pgc.state.pa.us or www.mckeever.org for more information.

**Contact Information:**
Pennsylvania Game Commission, Northwest Region
P.O. Box 31
Franklin, PA 16323
(814) 432-3187

Maurice K. Goddard State Park
684 Lake Wilhelm Road
Sandy Lake, PA 16145
(724) 253-4833

McKeever Environmental Learning Center
55 McKeever Lane
Sandy Lake, PA 16145
(724) 376-1000

Canvasback

# Somerset County

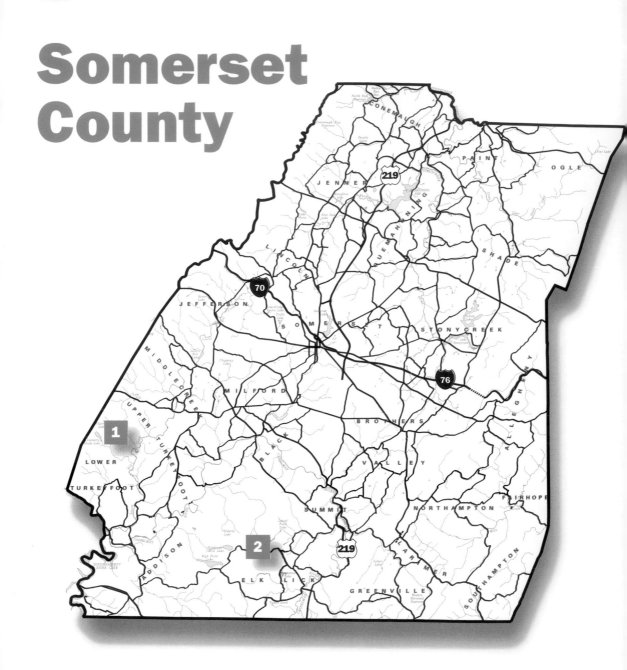

## Legend

 Handicapped Accessibility

 Hiking Trails

 Biking Trails

 Restrooms

 Dogs Allowed

# 1 CRANBERRY GLADE LAKE

**Location:** Cranberry Glade Lake is located in Somerset County, south of the town of Donegal and near the Fayette County border.

**Owner/Manager:** Commonwealth of Pennsylvania/ Pennsylvania Fish and Boat Commission.

**GPS Coordinates:** 39° 54' 24" N, 79° 22' 10" W

**Directions, Access, & Parking:** From I-76/ Pennsylvania Turnpike, take the Donegal exit. Follow PA-381 south to Normalville. Then take PA-653 east for 5 miles. Turn right and drive approximately 2 miles to Cranberry Road on the left, and follow it to the lake. To get to the wetlands, park at the parking/ boat launch area at the south end of the lake, walk across the dam, and follow the trail to the wetland's edge. Parking is available for cars.

**Site Description:** Cranberry Glade Lake is home to deciduous and coniferous forests, shrub/scrub, cultivated fields, marsh, lake, and stream areas. Canoeing is recommended to get close to the wetland areas located at the north end of the lake. The lake is only an average of four feet deep.

**Site Information:** Free admission. On-site restrooms. A trail at the south end of the lake connects to the Laurel Highlands Hiking Trail. Other trails traverse the surrounding State Game Lands 111. Canoeing/kayaking, boating (electric and non-powered only), and hunting are permitted. Lodging, restaurants, gasoline, and convenience stores are located nearby.

**Key Birds and Wildlife:** Alder Flycatcher, Northern Waterthrush, Canada Warbler, Osprey, American Black Duck. A variety of nesting songbirds can be found in the hemlocks at the north and south ends of the lake including Blue-headed Vireo, Veery, Hermit Thrush, Chestnut-sided Warbler, Magnolia Warbler, Black-throated Blue Warbler, Black-throated Green Warbler, Louisiana Waterthrush, and Swamp Sparrow. Primary fish in the lake include largemouth bass, bluegill, black crappie, yellow perch, northern pike, and a few trophy-size muskie.

**Other Comments:** Large wind turbines on site may detract from the natural experience. Ohiopyle State Park is about 10 miles away. Visit www.fishandboat.com/water/ lakes/cranberry_glade/00cranberry for more information.

**Contact Information:**
PA Fish and Boat Commission
Southwest Region Office
236 Lake Road
Somerset, PA 15501
(814) 445-8974

*Tree Swallow*

# 2 MOUNT DAVIS AND HIGH POINT LAKE

**Location:** Mount Davis is located within Forbes State Forest in Somerset County, east of the town of Meyersdale and just north of the Maryland border. High Point Lake is less than 5 miles west of Mount Davis.

**Owner/Manager:** Commonwealth of Pennsylvania/Pennsylvania Department of Conservation and Natural Resources; Pennsylvania Fish and Boat Commission

**GPS Coordinates:** 39° 47' 38" N, 79° 10' 0" W (Mt. Davis); 39° 46' 57" N, 79° 12' 45" W (High Point Lake)

**Directions, Access, & Parking:** Mount Davis: From the Somerset exit of I-76/PA Turnpike, follow US-219 south past the business exit to Meyersdale. At the American Legion Post in Meyersdale, turn right onto Broadway Street and then right onto Mt. Davis Road (SR2004). This will wind up to the summit. The parking area will be on the left. A trailhead to the southern part of the forest begins at the parking lot. Parking is available for cars. High Point Lake: From Mount Davis summit drive north to the intersection with Mt. Davis Road, and turn left onto Mt. Davis Road. Pass the road to Deer Valley Lake and turn right onto Lake Shore Road to reach the north shore access to High Point Lake. Farther along Mt. Davis Road you will reach the south shore access to the lake.

**Site Description:** Mount Davis, a secluded forest and the highest point in Pennsylvania at 3,213 feet, is home to deciduous, coniferous, and early successional forests, shrub/scrub, cultivated and fallow fields, and streams.

**Site Information:** Free admission. Nine hiking trails, an observation tower, restrooms, and interpretive signs are available. Canoeing/kayaking and boating with electric motors are permitted at nearby High Point Lake. Camping is limited to backpack-type camping. Lodging, restaurants, gasoline, and convenience stores are located nearby.

**Key Birds and Wildlife:** Ruffed Grouse, Whip-poor-will, Blue-headed Vireo, Common Raven, Brown Creeper, Winter Wren, Golden-crowned Kinglet, Veery, Hermit Thrush, Chestnut-sided Warbler, Magnolia Warbler, Black-throated Green Warbler, Black-throated Blue Warbler, Canada Warbler, Dark-eyed Junco, Rose-breasted Grosbeak, Bobolink, Grasshopper Sparrow, Purple Finch, Northern Saw-whet Owl, Blackburnian Warbler, Northern Waterthrush. The area boasts hemlock-lined streams, mountain laurel thickets, and conifer plantations that attract a wide variety of nesting songbirds. The fallow fields and reclaimed strip mines to the east are good locations for spotting grassland birds. High Point Lake to the west is worth a visit for waterfowl in migration. Black bear and timber rattlesnakes are in the area. High Point Lake has largemouth and smallmouth bass, walleye, northern pike, yellow perch, black crappie, bluegill, and brown bullhead.

**Other Comments:** When driving watch for Amish buggies which share the road. Expect high winds and low temperatures at the summit. Look for the unusual circular patterns of stone at the base of the observation tower; these were formed by the action of frost over thousands of years. Visit www.dcnr.state.pa.us/info/hikeforhealth for more information.

**Contact Information:**
Forbes State Forest
P.O. Box 519
Laughlintown, PA 15655
(724) 238-1200

*Short-eared Owl*

*Red-throated Loon*

# Venango County

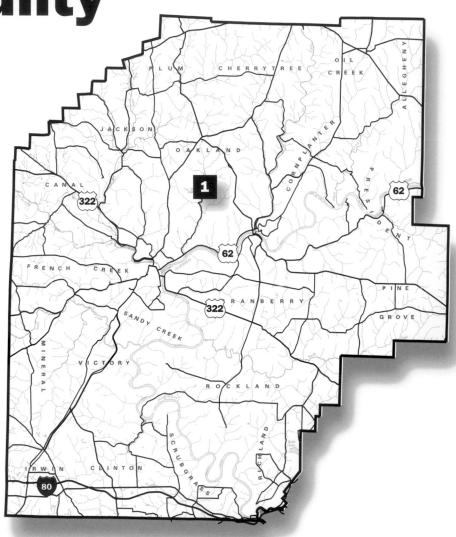

## Legend

 Handicapped Accessibility

 Hiking Trails

 Biking Trails

 Restrooms

 Dogs Allowed

# 1 TWO MILE RUN COUNTY PARK     

**Location:** Two Mile Run Park is located in Venango County, near the cities of Franklin and Oil City.

**Owner/Manager:** Venango County/Two Mile Run County Park Department

**GPS Coordinates:** 41° 28' 38" N, 79° 46' 7" W

**Directions, Access, & Parking:** The park is located at 471 Beach Road in Franklin. From the town of Franklin, go north on US-322/Meadville Pike. Turn right onto PA-417/Rocky Grove Avenue. Turn right onto Baker Road, then left onto Cherry Tree Road. Turn right onto Beach Road and turn into the parking area. There is access for cars and buses and ample parking.

**Site Description:** Two Mile Run County Park is 2,695 acres and Justus Lake is 144 acres. The area contains deciduous forest and lake areas.

**Site Information:** Admission is free, but there is a fee for camping and beach use. Twenty miles of trails, information, and restrooms are available. Motor boating, canoeing/kayaking, biking, picnicking, cross-country skiing, fishing, and hunting are permitted. Gasoline, lodging, restaurants, and convenience/grocery stores are located nearby.

**Key Birds and Wildlife:** Ruffed Grouse, Common Loon, Green Heron, Osprey, Bald Eagle, Forster's Tern, Belted Kingfisher, Yellow-bellied Sapsucker, Pileated Woodpecker, Least Flycatcher, Blue-headed Vireo, Warbling Vireo, Red-eyed Vireo, Tree Swallow, Blue-gray Gnatcatcher, Eastern Bluebird, Swainson's Thrush, Wood Thrush, Blue-winged Warbler, Tennessee Warbler, Nashville Warbler, Chestnut-sided Warbler, Magnolia Warbler, Cape May Warbler, Black-throated Blue Warbler, Yellow-rumped Warbler, Black-throated Green Warbler, Blackburnian Warbler, Bay-breasted Warbler, Blackpoll Warbler, American Redstart, Ovenbird, Northern Waterthrush, Kentucky Warbler, Hooded Warbler, Scarlet Tanager, Eastern Towhee, Swamp Sparrow, White-throated Sparrow, Rose-breasted Grosbeak, Indigo Bunting, Baltimore Oriole, Purple Finch. White-tailed deer, black bear, and American beaver may also be found here.

**Other Comments:** Venango County recently took over management of this park; it had been privately owned. Visit www.twomilerun.net for more information.

**Contact Information:**
Two Mile Run County Park
471 Beach Road
Franklin, PA 16323
(814) 676-6116

*Least Flycatcher*

# Warren County

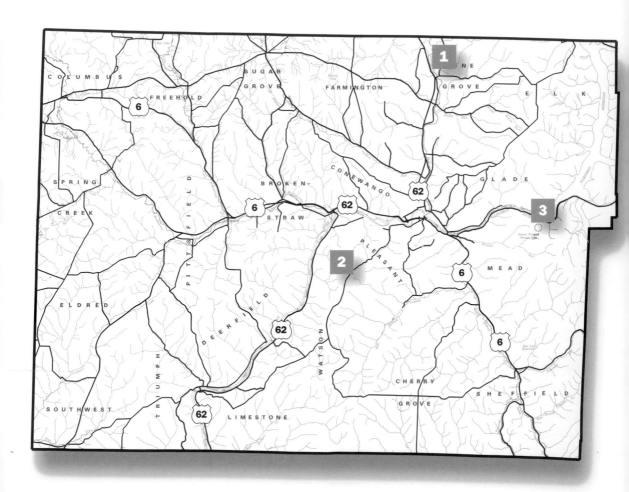

## Legend

 Handicapped Accessibility

 Hiking Trails

 Biking Trails

 Restrooms

 Dogs Allowed

## 1 AKELEY SWAMP
## STATE GAME LANDS 282

**Location:** Akeley Swamp is located in Warren County, just south of the New York State line and north of the town of Akeley.

**Owner/Manager:** Commonwealth of Pennsylvania/Pennsylvania Game Commission (500 acres); Northern Allegheny Conservation Association (40 acres)

**GPS Coordinates:** 41° 58' 50" N, 79° 8' 10" W

**Directions, Access, & Parking:** From the intersection of US-62 and PA-957 in Russell, go north on US-62 approximately 1.6 miles to Akeley. At Akeley turn right onto Cable Hollow Road and cross the bridge over Conewango Creek to Old US-62. Turn left onto Old US-62 and proceed approximately 1.3 miles. Turn left onto Martin Road. Follow Martin Road to a parking area at the end. A second parking area can be reached by following Old US-62 a little farther to Howard Road. Parking is available for cars and buses, and the venue is handicapped accessible.

**Site Description:** Akeley Swamp consists of approximately 500 acres of State Game Lands 282 and an adjacent parcel of 40 acres known as Mahaffey Wetlands Conservation Area. Included are a primary swamp of about 185 acres, three artificial ponds, shrub/scrub, marsh, and riparian areas. Vegetation of note includes floating pennywort and swamp white oak. Conewango Creek borders the western edge of the State Game Lands and the eastern edge of the conservation site. Akeley Swamp has been designated as Important Bird Area #15.

**Site Information:** Free admission. Horseback riding, mountain biking, motorized boating, canoeing/kayaking, cross-country skiing, hunting, trapping, and fishing are permitted. Restaurants, campgrounds, gasoline, and convenience stores are close by.

**Key Birds and Wildlife:** Least Bittern, Pied-billed Grebe, Virginia Rail, Sora, Common Moorhen, Black-throated Green Warbler, Blackburnian Warbler, Black-throated Blue Warbler, Canada Warbler, Mourning Warbler, Swainson's Thrush, Winter Wren, Swamp Sparrow. American Kestrel nest boxes have been monitored within the swamp. Spring and fall migrations are good times to observe waterfowl, waders, raptors, shorebirds, and warblers. Crossbills may be found during the winter. At least 147 avian species have been recorded at Akeley Swamp. This is also important habitat for the spiny softshell turtle and northern pike.

**Other Comments:** Akeley Swamp is located about 10 miles west of the Allegheny National Forest. It is only about 15 miles south of the Roger Tory Peterson Institute in Jamestown, NY. Visit www.pgc.state.pa.us for more information.

**Contact Information:**
Pennsylvania Game Commission, Northwest Region
P.O. Box 31
Franklin, PA 16323
(814) 432-3187

Northern Allegheny Conservation Association
P.O. Box 661
Warren, PA 16365

*Common Moorhen*

*Bufflehead*

# 2 ALLEGHENY NATIONAL FOREST: HEART'S CONTENT RECREATION AREA

**Location:** Heart's Content Recreation Area is situated within Allegheny National Forest. It is east of the town of Tidioute and southwest of the City of Warren in Warren County.

**Owner/Manager:** United States/United States Department of Agriculture Forest Service

**GPS Coordinates:** 41° 41' 31" N, 79° 15' 12" W

**Directions, Access, & Parking:** From US-6 (south of Warren), Heart's Content is about 15 miles to the southwest. Follow Pleasant Road (SR3005) south for 10.7 miles. When Pleasant Road becomes Heart's Content Road (SR2002), continue for 3.7 miles to the recreation area (portions are unpaved). The campground will be on the right, and the scenic area will be on the left. Parking is available for cars and buses in the scenic area. Facilities in the day-use area are handicapped accessible.

**Site Description:** The 122-acre Heart's Content Recreation Area contains deciduous and mixed forests and streams. Understory vegetation consists of ferns with some grasses, sedges, and wildflowers. This remote area includes an old-growth forest and is adjacent to a wilderness area. Some eastern hemlock, white pine, and American beech trees in the area are estimated to be 300–400 years old. There are steep hillsides with rock ledges and boulders. Heart's Content Recreation Area and the adjacent Hickory Creek Wilderness have been designated Important Bird Area #17.

**Site Information:** Free admission. Information and interpretive signs are provided. Horseback riding, mountain biking, cross-country skiing, snowmobiling, hunting, fishing, and picnicking are permitted. Campsites for families and groups and a playground are available. A scenic interpretive trail winds about a mile through a stand of timber. A 6.4-mile trail forms several loops for cross-country skiing. The 11-mile Hickory Creek Wilderness loop weaves through rolling terrain. A self-guided orienteering course provides an introduction to the sport.

**Key Birds and Wildlife:** Yellow-bellied Sapsucker, Blue-headed Vireo, Red-breasted Nuthatch, Brown Creeper, Winter Wren, Swainson's Thrush, Hermit Thrush, Nashville Warbler, Magnolia Warbler, Pine Warbler, Mourning Warbler, Canada Warbler. Seventy species of birds have been recorded here for the Pennsylvania Breeding Bird Atlas, including 16 species of warblers. Heart's Content boasts birds more common to Canada than to western Pennsylvania. Mammals include white-tailed deer, black bear, and northern water shrew.

**Other Comments:** An area saved from logging in the mid-1800s and the additional acreage surrounding it were designated as a Scenic Area in 1934. In 1936, the Civilian Conservation Corps built the pavilions and campground at Heart's Content. The Secretary of the Interior dedicated the Scenic Area as a National Natural Landmark in 1977 in order to encourage the conservation of this outstanding example of natural history. Visit www.fs.fed.us/r9/forests/allegheny for more information.

**Contact Information:**
Allegheny National Forest
4 Farm Colony Drive
Warren, PA 16365
(814) 723-5150

*Northern Mockingbird*

## 3 ALLEGHENY RESERVOIR AND KINZUA DAM

**Location:** Allegheny National Forest spreads through Warren, McKean, Forest, and Elk counties. In the heart of the forest but managed as separate entities, Kinzua Dam and the Pennsylvania section of Allegheny Reservoir are almost completely limited to northeastern Warren County. Some of the trails and scenic drives stretch into northwestern McKean County.

**Owner/Manager:** United States/United States Army Corps of Engineers

**GPS Coordinates:** 41° 50' 21" N, 79° 0' 23" W (parking lot below the dam)

**Directions, Access, & Parking:** From Warren, pick up US-6 or Business US-6 and follow either of these roads east to PA-59 (Kinzua Road). Follow PA-59 for 5.9 miles. Turn left onto Powerhouse Road and follow it to a large parking lot. Parking is available for cars and buses, and the site is handicapped accessible.

**Site Description:** Kinzua Dam, a concrete dam and earthen embankment, is 1,877 feet long and rises 179 feet above the river. Allegheny Reservoir is about 25 miles long and has an average depth of 48 feet but can reach a maximum of 132 feet. In the summer, it has an area of 12,080 acres. The dam and reservoir are surrounded by mature deciduous and mixed mature forests.

**Site Information:** Free admission. Miles of hiking trails, including part of the North Country Trail, crisscross the forest, mainly to the east of the reservoir. Several scenic overlooks, observation deck, visitor centers, boat launch ramps, playground, fish hatchery, restrooms, drinking water, and environmental education programs are available around the perimeter of the reservoir. For a scenic drive, take PA-59 and Longhouse Scenic Drive to the south and PA-321 to the east of the reservoir; views with fall foliage can be breathtaking. Motorized boating, canoeing/kayaking, snowmobiling, ATVing, and hunting are permitted. Restaurants, campgrounds, gasoline, and convenience stores are close by.

**Key Birds and Wildlife:** Wild Turkey, Northern Goshawk, Common Raven, Mourning Warbler, Magnolia Warbler, Blackburnian Warbler, Saw-whet Owl. A bird-viewing platform is set up below the dam for watching nesting Bald Eagles and Osprey feeding. A wide variety of waterfowl can be found on the reservoir.

**Other Comments:** Kinzua Dam was designed for flood control, navigation, power generation, recreation, and pollution abatement. Since 1965, the dam has prevented an estimated $360 million in flood damage. A recorded message at (814) 726-0164 gives updated lake and recreation information. Visit www.lrp.usace.army.mil/rec/rec.htm for more information.

**Contact Information:**
Kinzua Dam
1205 Kinzua Road
Warren, PA 16365
(814) 726-0661

Big Bend Visitor Center
(814) 726-0678

Allegheny National Fish Hatchery
Route 1, P.O. Box 1050
Warren, PA 16365
(814) 726-0890

Osprey

# Washington County

## Legend

 Handicapped Accessibility

 Hiking Trails

 Biking Trails

 Restrooms

 Dogs Allowed

## 1 BAVINGTON STATE GAME LANDS 432
### (ALSO KNOWN AS HILLMAN STATE PARK)

**Location:** Bavington State Game Lands 432, also known as Hillman State Park, is located in northern Washington County, west of Greater Pittsburgh International Airport and the City of Pittsburgh.

**Owner/Manager:** Commonwealth of Pennsylvania/ leased by the Pennsylvania Department of Conservation and Natural Resources to the Pennsylvania Game Commission to manage hunting

**GPS Coordinates:** 40° 26' 9" N, 80° 24' 23" W (entrance at Haul Road)

**Directions, Access, & Parking:** From Pittsburgh, take US-22 W to the Bavington exit. At the end of the ramp, turn right and then turn quickly left onto Old Steubenville Pike. Drive 3.4 miles on Steubenville Pike and make a right onto Haul Road. Park cars in the lot on the left side of Steubenville Pike to observe the nearby grasslands first. Drive on Haul Road and make stops along the way to check the old fields, upland brush, and pine groves. Return to Steubenville Pike and turn left. Drive about 1 mile. There will be a State Game Lands sign on the left. Immediately after the sign, turn left onto Knowlton Hill Road (this is a gravel road). Go 0.7 miles and stop to walk the Pitch Pine Trail loop through white pine, pitch pine, and bur oak forests. Continue on Knowlton Hill Road and make a right onto Kramer Road to return to Steubenville Pike. Make a left onto Steubenville Pike to return to US-22.

**Site Description:** Bavington State Game Lands covers 3,654 acres of undeveloped, rolling terrain averaging 600–800 feet in elevation. Many roads and trails lead through it. Dominant habitats are deciduous and coniferous forests, thickets of invasive shrubs, grassy fields, and steep eroding slopes. Near the creek, spring wildflowers include trillium, Virginia bluebells, and harbinger-of-spring. State Game Lands 432 is part of Important Bird Area #13.

**Site Information:** Free admission. Many on-site trails are available with varying degrees of difficulty. Mountain biking, horseback riding, cross-country skiing, model airplane flying, and hunting are permitted. Restaurants, lodging, and convenience/grocery stores are located nearby. Camping is available about 5 miles away in Raccoon Creek State Park.

**Key Birds and Wildlife:** American Woodcock, Whip-poor-will, Hermit Thrush, Northern Harrier, Ruffed Grouse, Louisiana Waterthrush, Blue-winged Warbler, Ovenbird, Prairie Warbler, Grasshopper Sparrow, Henslow's Sparrow, Golden-crowned Kinglet. This is a great area for migrant warblers in the spring. Five Point Road, located off Haul Road, is especially good for Tennessee Warbler and Wilson's Warbler. The coniferous stands are home to rare county breeders such as Red-breasted Nuthatch, Pine Warbler, and Barred Owl. During the winter the area has the potential for winter finches in influx years. Evening Grosbeak, Common Redpoll, and White-winged Crossbill have all been reported in the area. White-tailed deer and red fox may be seen. Spotted Wintergreen grows here.

**Other Comments:** This park is strictly carry-in/carry-out. Hillman State Park was a group of abandoned strip mines before it was donated to the state in 1996; this accounts for the unusual contours in the terrain. Stay on the trails to avoid ticks. For your safety, wear blaze orange or only hike on Sundays during hunting seasons. Visit www.dcnr.state.pa.us/ stateparks or www.pgc.state.pa.us/pgc for more information.

**Contact Information:**
Hillman State Park
c/o Raccoon Creek State Park
3000 State Route 18
Hookstown, PA 15050-9416
(724) 899-2200

Pennsylvania Game Commission, Southwest Region
4820 Route 711
Bolivar, PA 15923
(724) 238-9523

## 2 STATE GAME LANDS 232:    LOWER BUFFALO CREEK WATERSHED/GREEN COVE WETLAND

**Location:** Lower Buffalo Creek Watershed/Green Cove Wetland is located in Washington County, near the City of Washington.

**Owner/Manager:** Commonwealth of Pennsylvania/ Pennsylvania Game Commission

**GPS Coordinates:** 40° 11' 32" N, 80° 23' 33" W

**Directions, Access, & Parking:** From Washington, Pa. take I-70 W to PA-221/Taylorstown Exit 11. At the end of the ramp turn left, drive 0.1 miles to a stop sign, and then turn right onto PA-221 north (Buffalo Creek Road). Parking for SGL 232 is in several locations along Buffalo Creek Road. Continue on PA-221 N for 5.8 miles and turn right onto Green Cove Road. Travel 0.2 miles to a parking lot on the right; additional parking is also available in several locations along Green Cove Road. Green Cove Wetland has a handicapped-accessible observation area.

**Site Description:** The 21,939-acre Lower Buffalo Creek Watershed is home to deciduous and mixed forests, early grassland/savanna, cultivated fields, fallow fields, marsh, riparian, and stream areas. This site is an exceptional representative of high-quality riparian forest, and Buffalo Creek and its tributaries have especially high water quality. Green Cove Wetland was created in 2003; the project has successfully resulted in feeding and breeding habitat for many species. State Game Lands 232 covers a part of the Lower Buffalo Creek Watershed and the recently acquired Green Cove Wetlands for a total of 5,265 acres. This area has been designated as Important Bird Area #80.

**Site Information:** Free admission. Lodging, restaurants, gasoline, and convenience stores are nearby in Washington.

**Key Birds and Wildlife:** This is a great birding location any time during the year. In the spring, when water is present in the wetland area, Wood Duck, Green Heron, and Great Blue Heron are regulars. Shorebirds may be present along with American Bitterns in late April/early May. During the summer, breeding birds include Wood Duck, Willow Flycatcher, Yellow-breasted Chat, and Orchard Oriole. Overall, the Lower Buffalo Creek Watershed is home to over 100 species of birds during the breeding season and is a stopover area for many other species of Neotropical migrants in the spring. The area contains 51 active Great Blue Heron nests and a large concentration of Acadian Flycatchers, Cerulean Warblers, Louisiana Waterthrushes, and Yellow-throated Warblers. Fall can be spectacular at Green Cove with some of the highest concentrations of sparrows in the entire state. Swamp Sparrow numbers have reached triple digits, while Lincoln's Sparrow numbers can easily reach double digits. Rarities found at Green Cove in the fall have included Clay-colored Sparrow, Nelson's Sparrow, Dickcissel, and Sedge Wren. During the winter a few holdover Swamp Sparrows are usually around along with a few Fox Sparrows. The fields sometimes have Horned Larks or possibly a Northern Harrier.

**Other Comments:** A watershed rated "High Quality" by the Pennsylvania Department of Environmental Protection and the United States Environmental Protection Agency makes this corner of the Commonwealth a great place to enjoy the natural world. Visit www.pgc.state.pa.us for more information.

**Contact Information:**
Pennsylvania Game Commission, Southwest Region
4820 Route 711
Bolivar, PA 15923
(724) 238-9523

## 3 STATE GAME LANDS 302 🚶 🚲 🐕
## ENLOW FORK NATURAL AREA

**Location:** State Game Lands 302 is located at the border of Washington and Greene counties, along the Enlow Fork of Wheeling Creek.

**Owner/Manager:** Commonwealth of Pennsylvania/ Pennsylvania Game Commission

**GPS Coordinates:** 39° 57' 40" N, 80° 27' 42" W

**Directions, Access, & Parking:** From Washington, Pa, take I-70 W for about 10 miles toward Wheeling. Take Exit 6/PA-231 toward Claysville. Turn right at the end of the ramp onto PA-3024 (signs for Claysville). Immediately turn right at National Road/US-40. Go 0.7 miles and make a right at Bell Avenue/East Finley Drive/PA-231. Continue on East Finley Drive for 3.5 miles. Read the signs at intersections; your road may not be the one that is straight ahead. Turn right at Burnsville Ridge Road and follow it for 8 miles (reading street signs). Turn left at West Finley Road and go 2.5 miles. Turn right at Walker Hill Road and go 1.7 miles. Make a sharp right at Smokey Row Road and continue downhill for more than 1 mile until you reach the bottom of the valley. Parking is available for 5–10 cars, and there is a dirt road access.

**Site Description:** The 1,000-acre State Game Lands 302 is a mature, bottomland riparian habitat containing deciduous and early successional forests, cultivated and fallow fields, marsh, lake, and stream areas. It is known for its abundance of spring wildflowers. Enlow Fork has been designated as Important Bird Area #14.

**Site Information:** Free admission. Hiking trails may be grassy or muddy, depending on the season. Fishing, birding, and boating occur. Hunting is permitted.

**Key Birds and Wildlife:** Cerulean Warbler, Yellow-throated Warbler, Kentucky Warbler, Louisiana Waterthrush, Orchard Oriole, Acadian Flycatcher, Summer Tanager. This is a good area to find migrant passerines. Butterflies and dragonflies can be abundant.

**Other Comments:** State Game Lands 302 surrounds about 4.5 miles of the Enlow Fork of Wheeling Creek, which creates a rich riparian habitat. Visit www.pgc.state.pa.us for more information.

**Contact Information:**
Pennsylvania Game Commission, Southwest Region
4820 Route 711
Bolivar, PA 15923
(724) 238-9523

Gray Catbird

# Westmoreland County

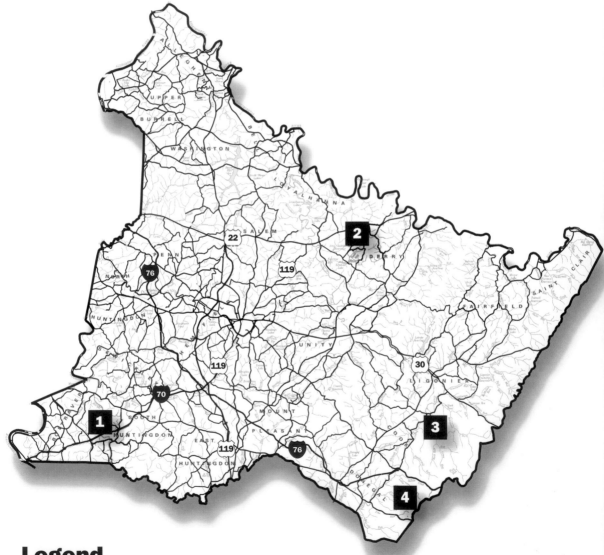

## Legend

 Handicapped Accessibility

 Hiking Trails

 Biking Trails

 Restrooms

 Dogs Allowed

## 1 CEDAR CREEK      COUNTY PARK

**Location:** Cedar Creek County Park is located in Westmoreland County, near the town of Belle Vernon.

**Owner/Manager:** Westmoreland County/Westmoreland County Bureau of Parks and Recreation

**GPS Coordinates:** 40° 10' 2" N, 79° 46' 11" W

**Directions, Access, & Parking:** From Pittsburgh, travel PA-51 south. At 10 miles past the bridge over the Monongahela River in Elizabeth, turn left at the traffic light (marked Concord Lane) and after 100 feet make a right onto Concord Lane. Travel 0.2 miles and turn left onto Lynn Road; continue for another 0.1 miles and turn right onto Port Royal Road. There is easy access and plenty of parking for cars and available parking for buses. Overnight parking is also available for trail users. The location is handicapped accessible.

**Site Description:** Cedar Creek County Park contains 464 acres of deciduous forest, shrub/scrub, fallow fields, river and stream areas. The Cedar Creek Gorge is located at the northern end of the park and is unique for its trillium and other wildflowers.

**Site Information:** Free admission. Information, interpretive trails, hiking and biking on the Youghiogheny River Trail, handicapped-accessible restrooms, camping, and drinking water are available. Bike rentals, a concession stand, and a boat launch are available at Cedar Creek Station. Mountain biking, leashed pets, horseback riding, motorized boating, and canoeing/kayaking are allowed. Portions of the park are open to hunting. A Model Radio Controlled Airfield also operates out of Cedar Creek Park. Lodging, restaurants, gasoline, and convenience stores are located nearby.

**Key Birds and Wildlife:** Yellow-throated Warbler, Louisiana Waterthrush, Orchard Oriole, Great Blue Heron, Green Heron, Killdeer, American Woodcock, Yellow-billed Cuckoo, Chimney Swift, Belted Kingfisher, Least Flycatcher, Warbling Vireo, White-eyed Vireo, Barn Swallow, Blue-gray Gnatcatcher, American Redstart, Indigo Bunting, Bobolink, Baltimore Oriole.

**Other Comments:** The Youghiogheny River Trail is part of the Great Allegheny Passage, a regional trail system that links Pittsburgh with Washington, D.C. From the northern part of the park, there is a breathtaking view of the deep gorge cut by the river. Visit www.inwestmoreland.com for more information.

**Contact Information:**
Cedar Creek County Park
305 Port Royal Drive
Belle Vernon, PA 15012

Westmoreland County Parks & Recreation
194 Donohoe Road
R.D. #12, Box 203
Greensburg, PA 15601
(724) 830-3950

*Carolina Chickadee*

# 2 KEYSTONE STATE PARK

**Location:** Keystone State Park is situated in Westmoreland County, near the towns of New Alexandria and Latrobe.

**Owner/Manager:** Commonwealth of Pennsylvania/ Pennsylvania Department of Conservation and Natural Resources

**GPS Coordinates:** 40° 22' 31" N, 79° 22' 45" W

**Directions, Access, & Parking:** The park is in Derry Township, 3 miles south of the intersection of PA-981 and US-22. The park office is on SR1018 (Keystone Park Road). From Pittsburgh take I-376 E towards Monroeville; the highway becomes US-22 E. Continue for 18 miles, turn right (south) onto PA-981 at New Alexandria. Travel on PA-981 for approximately 2 miles and turn left onto East Derry Street/ SR1018. Watch for park signs. Additional entrances can be found along PA-981. Parking is available for cars and buses. This site is also handicapped accessible.

**Site Description:** Keystone State Park has 1,200 acres, 78 of which form Keystone Lake. The park contains deciduous and coniferous forests, shrub/scrub, marsh, lake, and stream areas. Wildflowers including hepatica, spring beauty, bloodroot, cut-leaved toothwort, trout lily, and rue anemone grow in the park.

**Site Information:** Free admission. A visitor center located in the campground area offers an introduction to the history, flora, and fauna of the park. The visitor center also provides a bird checklist and other environmental materials. Six miles of trails loop through the park; all are rated easy to moderate. Trails are designated for foot traffic only, except one that is open to bikes. An observation deck, restrooms, drinking water, guided tours, environmental education programs, custom programs, and interpretive signage are available. Horseback riding, mountain biking, motor boating (electric), canoeing/kayaking, swimming, snowmobiling, hunting, fishing, and dog training are permitted. Camping is available in the park; lodging, restaurants, gasoline, and convenience stores are nearby.

**Key Birds and Wildlife:** Eastern Kingbird, Cedar Waxwing, Barn Swallow, Tree Swallow, Northern Rough-winged Swallow, Baltimore Oriole, Green Heron, Killdeer, Wood Duck, Red-eyed Vireo, Hooded Warbler, Kentucky Warbler, American Redstart, Cerulean Warbler, Eastern Phoebe, Acadian Flycatcher, Eastern Wood-Pewee, Red-bellied Woodpecker, Pileated Woodpecker, Broad-winged Hawk. American Beaver can be seen here.

**Other Comments:** Below the dam, a series of wayside exhibits shows how abandoned mine drainage seeping from Salem Mine #2 is being processed into cleaner water and returned to McCune Run. Visit www.dcnr.state.pa.us/stateparks for more information.

**Contact Information:**
Keystone State Park
1150 Keystone Park Road
Derry, PA 15627
(724) 668-2939

*American Goldfinch*

**3** **LINN RUN STATE PARK,**
**LAUREL SUMMIT STATE**
**PARK, SPRUCE FLATS BOG**

**Location:** Linn Run State Park, Laurel Summit State Park, and Spruce Flats Bog in Forbes State Forest are located on the boundary between Westmoreland and Somerset counties, near the town of Rector.

**Owner/Manager:** Commonwealth of Pennsylvania/ Pennsylvania Department of Conservation and Natural Resources and DCNR Bureau of Forestry

**GPS Coordinates:** 40° 10' 31 N, 79° 14' 13" W (Linn Run State Park); 40° 6' 56" N, 79° 10' 31 W (Laurel Summit State Park); 40° 7' 18" N, 79° 10' 29" W (Spruce Flats Bog)

**Directions, Access, & Parking:** Linn Run State Park: From I-76/Pennsylvania Turnpike, take the Donegal exit and follow PA-711 south to PA-381. Turn north onto PA-381 towards Rector, and turn right to head up the mountain on Linn Run Road. Parking is available for cars and buses, and the venue is handicapped accessible. Spruce Flats Bog: After exploring Linn Run State Park, travel southeast on Linn Run Road about 4 miles to Laurel Summit State Park to access the Spruce Flats Bog and Wolf Rocks trails.

**Site Description:** The gorgeous 612-acre Linn Run State Park is home to deciduous, coniferous, and mixed forests. There are steep mountain streams, Adams Falls, and abundant wildflowers. Look for mountain laurel and rhododendron blooming in the spring. Laurel Summit State Park covers 6 acres and reaches an elevation of 2,739 feet. Laurel Summit provides access to the adjacent Spruce Flats Wildlife Management Area, a 305-acre tract being developed to provide cover, food, and water for wildlife. Follow Bog Trail to Spruce Flats Bog, 28 acres noted for pitcher plant, sundew, cotton grass, large cranberry, and other plants more typical of plant communities farther north. Stay on the boardwalk and out of the bog to protect the unique plant species. From Laurel Summit you can also hike Wolf Rocks Trail, 1.75 miles each way, through deciduous, coniferous, and mixed deciduous forests and some open areas. The rocky overlook provides wide views along Laurel Ridge.

**Site Information:** Free admission. Hiking trails are available, but some are steep and rocky. Information, an observation deck, playgrounds, picnic areas, restrooms, and drinking water are on site. Mountain biking, snowmobiling, horseback riding, trapping, and hunting are permitted in state parks. Cabin rentals can be arranged.

**Key Birds and Wildlife:** Rose-breasted Grosbeak, Scarlet Tanager, Winter Wren, Acadian Flycatcher, Great Crested Flycatcher, Alder Flycatcher, Canada Warbler, Cerulean Warbler, Worm-eating Warbler, Black-throated Green Warbler, Black-throated Blue Warbler, Blackburnian Warbler, Hermit Thrush, Veery, Wild Turkey, Ruffed Grouse. Linn Run is an excellent trout stream. White-tailed deer and black bear are in the area.

**Other Comments:** Linn Run State Park is one of six state parks in a 25-mile stretch along Laurel Ridge straddling the boundary between Westmoreland, Fayette, and Somerset counties. Be prepared for colder temperatures due to the elevation. Visit www.dcnr.state.pa.us/stateparks, www.fay-west.com/westmoreland/laurelsummit/spruce-flats, for more information.

**Contact Information:**
Linn Run State Park
P.O. Box 50
Rector, PA 15677
(724) 238-6623

Laurel Summit State Park
c/o Linn Run State Park
(724) 238-6623

Forbes State Forest
(Spruce Flats Bog)
P.O. Box 519
Laughlintown, PA 15655
(724) 238-1200

# 4 POWDERMILL NATURE RESERVE

**Location:** Powdermill Nature Reserve is located in Westmoreland County, near the town of Ligonier.

**Owner/Manager:** Carnegie Museum of Natural History

**GPS Coordinates:** 40° 9' 36" N, 79° 16' 18" W

**Directions, Access, & Parking:** At the intersection of US-30 and PA-711 in Ligonier, take PA-711 south 3.3 miles to the Rector/Darlington intersection. There are signs there for Powdermill Nature Reserve and Linn Run State Park. Turn left toward Rector and go 1 mile. At the bottom of the hill, before going over the bridge, turn right onto PA-381 south. Follow PA-381 south for 3.3 miles to the Nature Reserve headquarters. Parking is available for cars and buses.

**Site Description:** Powdermill Nature Reserve is home to deciduous, mixed, and early successional forests, shrub/scrub, grassland/savanna, and riparian areas. Powdermill Nature Reserve has been designated as Important Bird Area #24.

**Site Information:** Free admission. On-site trails, a visitor center, restrooms, drinking water, guided tours, environmental education programs, custom educational programs, and interpretive signs are available. The new sustainably designed visitor center focuses on environmental education and houses several exhibits highlighting avian research conducted on site. These include the "marsh machine" wastewater treatment greenhouse, Golden Eagle satellite tracking display, and songbird banding program. Hunting is permitted.

**Key Birds and Wildlife:** Cerulean Warbler, Kentucky Warbler, Louisiana Waterthrush, Yellow-throated Warbler, Broad-winged Hawk, Yellow Warbler, White-eyed Vireo, Brown Thrasher, Field Sparrow, Indigo Bunting, Magnolia Warbler, Black-throated Blue Warbler, Blackpoll Warbler, Tennessee Warbler, Swainson's Thrush, Gray-checked Thrush, Dark-eyed Junco, Pine Siskin, Yellow-bellied Sapsucker, Pileated Woodpecker. This site is known for the incredible diversity of birds that stop over during both spring and fall migrations. There is also a large avian community that breeds on the reserve.

**Other Comments:** While driving watch for Amish buggies that share the road. The bird-banding station, one of the longest continually running programs in the country, is a must-see for visitors of all ages and all birding-skill levels. Visit www.powdermill.org for more information.

**Contact Information:**
Powdermill Nature Reserve
1847 Route 381
Rector, PA 15677
(724) 593-4070

*Yellow Warbler*

*Magnolia Warbler*

# Western Pennsylvania Birding List

1. Greater White-fronted Goose (Anser albifrons) Casual
2. Snow Goose (Chen caerulescens) Casual
3. Ross's Goose (Chen rossii) Casual
4. Brant (Branta bernicla) Regular Casual
5. Cackling Goose (Branta hutchinsii) Casual
6. Canada Goose (Branta canadensis) Regular
7. Mute Swan (Cygnus olor) Regular
8. Tundra Swan (Cygnus columbianus) Regular
9. Wood Duck (Aix sponsa) Regular
10. Gadwall (Anas strepera) Regular
11. Eurasian Wigeon (Anas penelope) Casual
12. American Wigeon (Anas americana) Regular
13. American Black Duck (Anas rubripes) Regular
14. Mallard (Anas platyrhynchos) Regular
15. Blue-winged Teal (Anas discors) Regular
16. Northern Shoveler (Anas clypeata) Regular
17. Northern Pintail (Anas acuta) Regular
18. Green-winged Teal (Anas crecca) Regular
19. Canvasback (Aythya valisineria) Regular
20. Redhead (Aythya americana) Regular
21. Ring-necked Duck (Aythya collaris) Regular
22. Tufted Duck (Aythya fuligula) Accidental
23. Greater Scaup (Aythya marila) Regular
24. Lesser Scaup (Aythya affinis) Regular
25. King Eider (Somateria spectabilis) Casual
26. Harlequin Duck (Histrionicus histrionicus) Casual
27. White-winged Scoter (Melanitta fusca) Regular
28. Surf Scoter (Melanitta perspicillata) Regular

Snow Goose

29. Black Scoter (Melanitta nigra) Regular
30. Long-tailed Duck (Clangula hyemalis) Regular
31. Bufflehead (Bucephala albeola) Regular
32. Common Goldeneye (Bucephala clangula) Regular
33. Barrow's Goldeneye (Bucephala islandica) Accidental
34. Hooded Merganser (Lophodytes cucullatus) Regular
35. Common Merganser (Mergus merganser) Regular
36. Red-breasted Merganser (Mergus serrator) Regular
37. Ruddy Duck (Oxyura jamaicensis) Regular
38. Ring-necked Pheasant (Phasianus colchicus) Regular
39. Ruffed Grouse (Bonasa umbellus) Regular
40. Wild Turkey (Meleagris gallopavo) Regular
41. Northern Bobwhite (Colinus virginianus) Regular
42. Red-throated Loon (Gavia stellata) Regular
43. Common Loon (Gavia immer) Regular
44. Pied-billed Grebe (Podilymbus podiceps) Regular
45. Horned Grebe (Podiceps auritus) Regular
46. Red-necked Grebe (Podiceps grisegena) Regular
47. Eared Grebe (Podiceps nigricollis) Casual

48. Leech's Storm Petrel (Oceanodroma leucorhoa) Accidental
49. American White Pelican (Pelecanus erythrorhynchos) Casual
50. Double-crested Cormorant (Phalacrocorax auritus) Regular
51. American Bittern (Botaurus lentiginosus) Regular
52. Least Bittern (Ixobrychus exilis) Regular
53. Great Blue Heron (Ardea herodias) Regular
54. Great Egret (Ardea alba) Regular
55. Snowy Egret (Egretta thula) Casual
56. Little Blue Heron (Egretta caerulea) Casual
57. Tricolored Heron (Egretta tricolor) Casual
58. Cattle Egret (Bubulcus ibis) Casual

Red-breasted Merganser

# Western Pennsylvania Birding List

59. Green Heron (Butorides virescens) Regular
60. Black-crowned Night-Heron (Nycticorax nycticorax) Regular
61. Yellow-crowned Night-Heron (Nyctanassa violacea) Accidental
62. Glossy Ibis (Plegadis falcinellus) Casual
63. Black Vulture (Coragyps atratus) Casual
64. Turkey Vulture (Cathartes aura) Regular
65. Osprey (Pandion haliaetus) Regular
66. Swallow-tailed Kite (Elanoides forficatus) Accidental
67. Mississippi Kite (Ictinia mississippiensis) Accidental
68. Bald Eagle (Haliaeetus leucocephalus) Regular
69. Northern Harrier (Circus cyaneus) Regular
70. Sharp-shinned Hawk (Accipiter striatus) Regular
71. Cooper's Hawk (Accipiter cooperii) Regular
72. Northern Goshawk (Accipiter gentilis) Regular
73. Red-shouldered Hawk (Buteo lineatus) Regular
74. Broad-winged Hawk (Buteo platypterus) Regular
75. Red-tailed Hawk (Buteo jamaicensis) Regular
76. Rough-legged Hawk (Buteo lagopus) Regular
77. Golden Eagle (Aquila chrysaetos) Regular
78. American Kestrel (Falco sparverius) Regular
79. Merlin (Falco columbarius) Regular
80. Gyrfalcon (Falco rusticolus) Accidental

Green Heron

81. Peregrine Falcon (Falco peregrinus) Regular
82. Yellow Rail (Coturnicops noveboracensis) Accidental
83. Black Rail (Laterallus jamaicensis) Accidental
84. Clapper Rail (Rallus longirostris) Accidental
85. King Rail (Rallus elegans) Casual
86. Virginia Rail (Rallus limicola) Regular
87. Sora (Porzana carolina) Regular
88. Purple Gallinule (Porphyrio martinica) Accidental
89. Common Moorhen (Gallinula chloropus) Regular
90. American Coot (Fulica americana) Regular

Virginia Rail

91. Sandhill Crane (Grus canadensis) Regular
92. Black-bellied Plover (Pluvialis squatarola) Regular
93. American Golden-Plover (Pluvialis dominica) Regular
94. Snowy Plover (Charadrius alexandrinus) Accidental
95. Wilson's Plover (Charadrius wilsonia) Accidental
96. Semipalmated Plover (Charadrius semipalmatus) Regular
97. Piping Plover (Charadrius melodus) Casual
98. Killdeer (Charadrius vociferus) Regular
99. American Oystercatcher (Haematopus palliatus) Accidental
100. Black-necked Stilt (Himantopus mexicanus) Accidental
101. American Avocet (Recurvirostra americana) Regular
102. Greater Yellowlegs (Tringa melanoleuca) Regular
103. Lesser Yellowlegs (Tringa flavipes) Regular
104. Solitary Sandpiper (Tringa solitaria) Regular
105. Willet (Tringa semipalmata) Regular
106. Spotted Sandpiper (Actitis macularius) Regular
107. Upland Sandpiper (Bartramia longicauda) Regular
108. Long-billed Curlew (Numenius americanus) Accidental
109. Whimbrel (Numenius phaeopus) Regular

# Western Pennsylvania Birding List

*Ruddy Turnstone*

110. Hudsonian Godwit (Limosa haemastica) Casual
111. Marbled Godwit (Limosa fedoa) Casual
112. Ruddy Turnstone (Arenaria interpres) Regular
113. Surfbird (Aphriza virgata) Accidental
114. Red Knot (Calidris canutus) Regular Casual
115. Sanderling (Calidris alba) Regular
116. Semipalmated Sandpiper (Calidris pusilla) Regular
117. Western Sandpiper (Calidris mauri) Casual
118. Least Sandpiper (Calidris minutilla) Regular
119. White-rumped Sandpiper (Calidris fuscicollis) Regular

120. Baird's Sandpiper (Calidris bairdii) Regular
121. Pectoral Sandpiper (Calidris melanotos) Regular
122. Purple Sandpiper (Calidris maritima) Casual
123. Dunlin (Calidris alpina) Regular
124. Stilt Sandpiper (Calidris himantopus) Regular
125. Buff-breasted Sandpiper (Tryngites subruficollis) Regular
126. Short-billed Dowitcher (Limnodromus griseus) Regular
127. Long-billed Dowitcher (Limnodromus scolopaceus) Regular
128. Wilson's Snipe (Gallinago delicata) Regular

129. American Woodcock (Scolopax minor) Regular
130. Wilson's Phalarope (Phalaropustricolor) Casual
131. Red-necked Phalarope (Phalaropus lobatus) Casual
132. Red Phalarope (Phalaropus fulicarius) Casual
133. Laughing Gull (Larus atricilla) Casual
134. Franklin's Gull (Larus pipixcan) Casual
135. Little Gull (Larus minutus) Regular
136. Black-headed Gull (Larus ridibundus) Casual
137. Bonaparte's Gull (Larus philadelphia) Regular
138. Ring-billed Gull (Larus delawarensis) Regular
139. California Gull (Larus californicus) Accidental
140. Herring Gull (Larus argentatus) Regular
141. Thayer's Gull (Larus thayeri) Casual
142. Iceland Gull (Larus glaucoides ) Regular
143. Lesser Black-backed Gull (Larus fuscus) Regular
144. Glaucous Gull (Larus hyperboreus) Regular
145. Great Black-backed Gull (Larus marinus) Regular
146. Sabine's Gull (Xema sabini) Casual
147. Black-legged Kittiwake (Rissa tridactyla) Casual
148. Caspian Tern (Hydroprogne caspia) Regular
149. Common Tern (Sterna hirundo) Regular
150. Arctic Tern (Sterna paradisaea) Accidental
151. Forster's Tern (Sterna forsteri) Regular
152. Least Tern (Sternula antillarum) Casual
153. Sooty Tern (Onychoprion fuscatus) Accidental
154. Black Tern (Chlidonias niger) Regular
155. Pomarine Jaeger (Stercorarius pomarinus) Casual
156. Parasitic Jaeger (Stercorarius parasiticus) Casual
157. Rock Pigeon (Columba livia) Regular
158. Eurasian Collared-Dove (Streptopelia decaocto) Casual
159. Mourning Dove (Zenaida macroura) Regular
160. Black-billed Cuckoo (Coccyzus erythropthalmus) Regular
161. Yellow-billed Cuckoo (Coccyzus americanus) Regular
162. Barn Owl (Tyto alba) Casual
163. Eastern Screech-Owl (Megascops asio) Regular
164. Great Horned Owl (Bubo virginianus) Regular
165. Snowy Owl (Bubo scandiacus) Casual
166. Northern Hawk Owl (Surnia ulula) Accidental
167. Barred Owl (Strix varia) Regular
168. Great Gray Owl (Strix nebulosa) Accidental
169. Long-eared Owl (Asio otus) Regular
170. Short-eared Owl (Asio flammeus) Regular
171. Boreal Owl (Aegolius funereus) Accidental
172. Northern Saw-whet Owl (Aegolius acadicus) Regular

# Western Pennsylvania Birding List

173. Common Nighthawk (Chordeiles minor) Regular
174. Chuck-wills-widow (Caprimulgus carolinesis) Accidental
175. Whip-poor-will (Caprimulgus vociferus) Regular
176. Chimney Swift (Chaetura pelagica) Regular
177. Ruby-throated Hummingbird (Archilochus colubris) Regular
178. Rufous Hummingbird (Selasphorus rufus) Casual
179. Belted Kingfisher (Megaceryle alcyon) Regular
180. Red-headed Woodpecker (Melanerpes erythrocephalus) Regular
181. Red-bellied Woodpecker (Melanerpes carolinus) Regular
182. Yellow-bellied Sapsucker (Sphyrapicus varius) Regular
183. Downy Woodpecker (Picoides pubescens) Regular
184. Hairy Woodpecker (Picoides villosus) Regular
185. Northern Flicker (Colaptes auratus) Regular
186. Pileated Woodpecker (Dryocopus pileatus) Regular
187. Olive-sided Flycatcher (Contopus cooperi) Regular
188. Eastern Wood-Pewee (Contopus virens) Regular
189. Yellow-bellied Flycatcher (Empidonax flaviventris) Regular
190. Acadian Flycatcher (Empidonax virescens) Regular
191. Alder Flycatcher (Empidonax alnorum) Regular
192. Willow Flycatcher (Empidonax traillii) Regular
193. Least Flycatcher (Empidonax minimus) Regular
194. Eastern Phoebe (Sayornis phoebe) Regular
195. Great Crested Flycatcher (Myiarchus crinitus) Regular
196. Western Kingbird (Tyrannus verticalis) Casual
197. Eastern Kingbird (Tyrannus tyrannus) Regular
198. Scissor-tailed Flycatcher (Tyrannus forficatus) Accidental
199. Loggerhead Shrike (Lanius ludovicianus) Casual
200. Northern Shrike (Lanius excubitor) Regular
201. White-eyed Vireo (Vireo griseus) Regular
202. Bell's Vireo (Vireo bellii) Accidental
203. Yellow-throated Vireo (Vireo flavifrons) Regular

204. Blue-headed Vireo (Vireo solitarius) Regular
205. Warbling Vireo (Vireo gilvus) Regular
206. Philadelphia Vireo (Vireo philadelphicus) Regular
207. Red-eyed Vireo (Vireo olivaceus) Regular
208. Blue Jay (Cyanocitta cristata) Regular
209. American Crow (Corvus brachyrhynchos) Regular
210. Fish Crow (Corvus ossifragus) Regular
211. Common Raven (Corvus corax) Regular
212. Horned Lark (Eremophila alpestris) Regular
213. Purple Martin (Progne subis) Regular
214. Tree Swallow (Tachycineta bicolor) Regular
215. Northern Rough-winged Swallow (Stelgidopteryx serripennis) Regular
216. Bank Swallow (Riparia riparia) Regular
217. Cliff Swallow (Petrochelidon pyrrhonota) Regular
218. Cave Swallow (Petrochelidon fulva) – Accidental

219. Barn Swallow (Hirundo rustica) Regular
220. Carolina Chickadee (Poecile carolinensis) Regular
221. Black-capped Chickadee (Poecile atricapillus) Regular
222. Boreal Chickadee (Poecile hudsonica) Accidental
223. Tufted Titmouse (Baeolophus bicolor) Regular
224. Red-breasted Nuthatch (Sitta canadensis) Regular
225. White-breasted Nuthatch (Sitta carolinensis) Regular
226. Brown Creeper (Certhia americana) Regular
227. Carolina Wren (Thryothorus ludovicianus) Regular
228. House Wren (Troglodytes aedon) Regular.
229. Winter Wren (Troglodytes troglodytes) Regular
230. Sedge Wren (Cistothorus platensis) Regular

*Rough-winged Swallow*

# Western Pennsylvania Birding List

231. Marsh Wren (Cistothorus palustris) Regular
232. Golden-crowned Kinglet (Regulus satrapa) Regular
233. Ruby-crowned Kinglet (Regulus calendula) Regular
234. Blue-gray Gnatcatcher (Polioptila caerulea) Regular
235. Eastern Bluebird (Sialia sialis) Regular
236. Townsend's Solitare (Myadestes townsendi) Accidental
237. Veery (Catharus fuscescens) Regular
238. Gray-cheeked Thrush (Catharus minimus) Regular
239. Bicknell's Thrush (Catharus bicknelli) Accidental
240. Swainson's Thrush (Catharus ustulatus) Regular
241. Hermit Thrush (Catharus guttatus) Regular
242. Wood Thrush (Hylocichla mustelina) Regular
243. American Robin (Turdus migratorius) Regular
244. Gray Catbird (Dumetella carolinensis) Regular
245. Northern Mockingbird (Mimus polyglottos) Regular
246. Brown Thrasher (Toxostoma rufum) Regular
247. European Starling (Sturnus vulgaris) Regular
248. American Pipit (Anthus rubescens) Regular
249. Bohemian Waxwing (Bombycilla garrulus) Casual
250. Cedar Waxwing (Bombycilla cedrorum) Regular
251. Blue-winged Warbler (Vermivora pinus) Regular
252. Golden-winged Warbler (Vermivora chrysoptera) Regular
253. Tennessee Warbler (Vermivora peregrina) Regular
254. Orange-crowned Warbler (Vermivora celata) Regular
255. Nashville Warbler (Vermivora ruficapilla) Regular
256. Northern Parula (Parula americana) Regular
257. Yellow Warbler (Dendroica petechia) Regular
258. Chestnut-sided Warbler (Dendroica pensylvanica) Regular
259. Magnolia Warbler (Dendroica magnolia) Regular
260. Cape May Warbler (Dendroica tigrina) Regular
261. Black-throated Blue Warbler (Dendroica caerulescens) Regular
262. Yellow-rumped Warbler (Dendroica coronata) Regular

263. Black-throated Green Warbler (Dendroica virens) Regular
264. Blackburnian Warbler (Dendroica fusca) Regular
265. Yellow-throated Warbler (Dendroica dominica) Regular
266. Pine Warbler (Dendroica pinus) Regular
267. Kirtland's Warbler (Dendroica kirtlandii) Accidental
268. Prairie Warbler (Dendroica discolor) Regular
269. Palm Warbler (Dendroica palmarum) Regular
270. Bay-breasted Warbler (Dendroica castanea) Regular
271. Blackpoll Warbler (Dendroica striata) Regular
272. Cerulean Warbler (Dendroica cerulea) Regular
273. Black-and-white Warbler (Mniotilta varia) Regular
274. American Redstart (Setophaga ruticilla) Regular
275. Prothonotary Warbler (Protonotaria citrea) Regular
276. Worm-eating Warbler (Helmitheros vermivorum) Regular
277. Swainson's Warbler (Limnothlypis swainsonii) Casual
278. Ovenbird (Seiurus aurocapilla) Regular
279. Northern Waterthrush (Seiurus noveboracensis) Regular
280. Louisiana Waterthrush (Seiurus motacilla) Regular
281. Kentucky Warbler (Oporornis formosus) Regular
282. Connecticut Warbler (Oporornis agilis) Regular
283. Mourning Warbler (Oporornis philadelphia) Regular
284. Common Yellowthroat (Geothlypis trichas) Regular
285. Hooded Warbler (Wilsonia citrina) Regular
286. Wilson's Warbler (Wilsonia pusilla) Regular
287. Canada Warbler (Wilsonia canadensis) Regular
288. Yellow-breasted Chat (Icteria virens) Regular
289. Summer Tanager (Piranga rubra) Casual
290. Scarlet Tanager (Piranga olivacea) Regular
291. Western Tanager (Piranga ludoviciana) Accidental
292. Eastern Towhee (Pipilo erythrophthalmus) Regular
293. American Tree Sparrow (Spizella arborea) Regular
294. Chipping Sparrow (Spizella passerina) Regular
295. Clay-colored Sparrow (Spizella pallida) Regular
296. Field Sparrow (Spizella pusilla) Regular
297. Vesper Sparrow (Pooecetes gramineus) Regular
298. Lark Sparrow (Chondestes grammacus) Accidental
299. Lark Bunting (Calamospiza melanocorys) Accidental
300. Savannah Sparrow (Passerculus sandwichensis) Regular

# Western Pennsylvania Birding List

**301.** Grasshopper Sparrow (Ammodramus savannarum) Regular

**302.** Henslow's Sparrow (Ammodramus henslowii) Regular

**303.** Le Conte's Sparrow (Ammodramus leconteii) Accidental

**304.** Nelson's Sparrow (Ammodramus nelsoni) Casual

**305.** Fox Sparrow (Passerella iliaca) Regular

**306.** Song Sparrow (Melospiza melodia) Regular

**307.** Lincoln's Sparrow (Melospiza lincolnii) Regular

**308.** Swamp Sparrow (Melospiza georgiana) Regular

**309.** White-throated Sparrow (Zonotrichia albicollis) Regular

**310.** Harris' Sparrow (Zonotrichia querula) Accidental

**311.** White-crowned Sparrow (Zonotrichia leucophrys) Regular

**312.** Dark-eyed Junco (Junco hyemalis) Regular

**313.** Lapland Longspur (Calcarius lapponicus) Regular

**314.** Snow Bunting (Plectrophenax nivalis) Regular

**315.** Northern Cardinal (Cardinalis cardinalis) Regular

**316.** Rose-breasted Grosbeak (Pheucticus ludovicianus) Regular

**317.** Black-headed Grosbeak (Pheucticus melanocephalus) Accidental

**318.** Indigo Bunting (Passerina cyanea) Regular

**319.** Painted Bunting (Passerina ciris) Accidental

**320.** Dickcissel (Spiza americana) Regular Casual

**321.** Bobolink (Dolichonyx oryzivorus) Regular

**322.** Red-winged Blackbird (Agelaius phoeniceus) Regular

**323.** Eastern Meadowlark (Sturnella magna) Regular

**324.** Western Meadowlark (Sturnella neglecta) Accidental

**325.** Yellow-headed Blackbird (Xanthocephalus xanthocephalus) Accidental

**326.** Rusty Blackbird (Euphagus carolinus) Regular

**327.** Brewer's Blackbird (Euphagus cyanocephalus) Casual

**328.** Common Crackle (Quiscalus quiscula) Regular

**329.** Brown-headed Cowbird (Molothrus ater) Regular

**330.** Orchard Oriole (Icterus spurius) Regular

331. Baltimore Oriole (Icterus galbula) Regular
332. Brambling (Fringilla montifringilla) Accidental
333. Pine Grosbeak (Pinicola enucleator) Casual
334. Purple Finch (Carpodacus purpureus) Regular
335. House Finch (Carpodacus mexicanus) Regular
336. Red Crossbill (Loxia curvirostra) Casual
337. White-winged Crossbill (Loxia leucoptera) Casual
338. Common Redpoll (Carduelis flammea) Casual
339. Hoary Redpoll (Carduelis hornemanni) Accidental
340. Pine Siskin (Carduelis pinus) Regular
341. American Goldfinch (Carduelis tristis) Regular
342. Evening Grosbeak (Coccothraustes vespertinus) Casual
343. House Sparrow (Passer domesticus) Regular

*Lincoln's Sparrow*

*Bald Knob*

Least Bittern